REVELATION
UNVEILED

"WHAT WAS, WHAT IS,
WHAT IS TO COME"

REVIVING THE CHURCH | REACHING THE LOST

JEHOVAH JIREH *ministries*
THE LORD WHO PROVIDES

First Edition: 2025
Revelation Unveiled / Dr. Ralph W. Jenkins
Paperback ISBN: 978-1-966923-02-2
eBook ISBN: 978-1-966923-03-9

CONTENTS

REVELATION
UNVEILED

DEDICATION

*To all who have chosen to journey through the pages of **Revelation Unveiled**, I dedicate this work to you. Your desire to seek, understand, and be transformed by God's Word is a reflection of the faithful pursuit we are all called to in Christ. May this devotional encourage you to see the wonder of God's sovereignty, the depth of His love, and the promise of His return.*

As you explore what was, what is, and what is to come, may your heart be drawn closer to the One who holds all things in His hands. My prayer is that this study strengthens your faith, deepens your love for Christ, and fills you with the hope of His glorious return.

May we all live expectantly, looking to the day when He will make all things new.

ACKNOWLEDGMENT

I would like to express my heartfelt gratitude to the men of faith whose profound writings and teachings have shaped my love for the study of end-time doctrine. Men like Tim LaHaye, John Hagee, David Jeremiah, Dwight Pentecost, John Walvoord, Adrian Rogers and others whose commentaries and insights have greatly influenced my understanding of the book of Revelation and the unfolding of God's prophetic plan. Most of these men are with our Lord today but their influence lives beyond them.

Their dedication to faithfully teaching the Word of God has inspired my own journey through the Scriptures and stirred a passion within me to share this study with others. It is because of their faithfulness in ministry that I, too, have come to cherish the study of Revelation: What was, What is, and What is to come.

Thank you all for being faithful stewards of God's truth and for igniting a love for His prophetic Word in so many of us.

Dr. Ralph W. Jenkins

PREFACE

The book of Revelation is one of the most awe-inspiring, challenging, and ultimately encouraging books of the Bible. It reveals the culmination of God's plan for humanity, the defeat of evil, and the triumphant reign of Christ. For believers, it is a book of hope, reminding us that no matter what happens in this world, God is in control. His victory is assured.

As we walk through the pages of Revelation, we will see both the present-day significance and the prophetic vision of what is to come. The seven churches addressed in chapters 2-3 are a mirror for us today calling us to examine our faith, our witness, and our relationship with Christ. Each of these churches also represents a period in church history, showing the progression of God's work throughout the ages.

In this devotional, we will follow a structure that helps us uncover the layers of this rich book. The rapture of the church, which I believe is prophetically symbolized in chapter 4, signals the beginning of the most dramatic time of tribulation the world has ever seen. Yet, through all the judgments, signs, and events of chapters 6-18, we will see God's redemptive hand at work. The book culminates with the glorious return of Christ in chapter 19 and the establishment of His eternal kingdom.

My prayer is that this devotional will not only deepen your understanding of Revelation but also strengthen your faith and bring hope for the future. No matter how dark the days may seem, we can look forward to the time when all things will be made new, and we will dwell with the Lord forever.

May this journey through the book of Revelation encourage your heart, equip your mind, and embolden your faith.

HOW TO USE
REVELATION UNVEILED

Welcome to *Revelation Unveiled*, a daily devotional journey through one of the most fascinating and powerful books in the Bible. This devotional is designed to help you both understand the prophetic truths of Revelation and grow deeper in your relationship with Jesus Christ. As you walk through this study, you'll encounter clear explanations, practical applications, and personal challenges to equip you in your daily life.

Here's how to get the most out of this devotional:

1.   START WITH PRAYER

Before you begin reading each day's devotion, take a moment to pray. Ask God to open your heart to His Word and to help you understand what He's revealing through the book of Revelation. Pray for wisdom, insight, and a willingness to apply the truths you'll encounter.

2.   READ THE SCRIPTURE

Each devotional begins with a passage from Revelation. Take the time to read these verses slowly and reflect on what God is saying. This will provide the foundation for the devotion and help you gain a deeper understanding of the book's themes.

3.   FOCUS ON THE ANECDOTE

The devotional starts with a relatable story or thought to help illustrate the deeper truths found in the passage. This will draw you into the message in a personal and engaging way, making the content more accessible and easier to relate to your life.

4.   UNDERSTAND THE EXPLANATION

After the anecdote, you'll find a section that explains the passage more deeply. Revelation can be challenging to understand, but this section will help break down key elements, focusing on what's happening in the text and how it fits into God's larger plan.

5.   APPLY THE TRUTH

Every devotion concludes with a practical application. These insights are meant to equip you to live in light of the truths revealed in Revelation. Consider how the passage can shape your actions, attitudes, and choices, and think about how you can apply these truths in your daily walk with Christ.

6.   PRAY FOR GROWTH

Each day, a prayer is provided to help you respond to what you've read. Use this as a guide, but feel free to expand it as the Holy Spirit leads. This is your opportunity to ask God to help you live out what you've learned.

7.   EMBRACE THE CHALLENGE

Each devotional ends with a challenge—something specific you can do in response to what you've learned. Whether it's reflecting on a question, taking a step of faith, or sharing your insights with someone else, these challenges are designed to help you grow spiritually and live with purpose.

8.   TAKE IT ONE DAY AT A TIME

The book of Revelation is deep, and it's easy to feel overwhelmed. That's why this devotional is designed to be taken one small step at a time, day by day. Don't rush through it. Give yourself time to reflect, pray, and process what you're learning.

9. BEYOND THE UNVEILING

At the end of each week there are a series of questions built to take you a little deeper into your study. Take time to answer these questions. They are intended to help you gain more understanding from the Book of Revelation and help you apply what you learn even further.

10. KEEP GOING

Revelation contains rich truths that will equip, encourage, and challenge you. Stay committed to the journey, even when it feels difficult. God has something special to reveal to you, and as you persevere, you'll grow in your understanding of His Word and His plan for the future.

AM I SAVED???

I have spent most of my Christian life sharing the Gospel of Christ. If I've learned one thing, it is to never assume someone knows Christ as the Lord of their life. If you know Christ as Lord, I praise God with you.

It may be that as you start this devotional that you are unsure if you are or are not saved. May I take time to present to you the gospel of Christ and how you can be saved, forgiven, and have a home in heaven that can be never be taken from you before you begin this devotional.

THE ROMAN ROAD TO SALVATION

SCRIPTURE READING:

- Romans 3:23 (NASB): "For all have sinned and fall short of the glory of God."
- Romans 6:23 (NASB): "For the wages of sin is death, but the gracious gift of God is eternal life in Christ Jesus our Lord."
- Romans 5:8 (NASB): "But God demonstrates His own love toward us, in that while we were still sinners, Christ died for us."
- Romans 10:9-10 (NASB): "That if you confess with your mouth Jesus as Lord, and believe in your heart that God raised Him from the dead, you will be saved; for with the heart a person believes, resulting in righteousness, and with the mouth he confesses, resulting in salvation."
- Romans 10:13 (NASB): "For everyone who calls on the name of the Lord will be saved."

DEVOTION:

The "Roman Road to Salvation" is a powerful and clear presentation of the gospel, drawn from key verses in the book of Romans. It walks us through the steps of recognizing our need for salvation, understanding God's solution, and responding to His offer of eternal life.

STEP 1: OUR CONDITION—ROMANS 3:23

The journey begins with a sobering truth: "For all have sinned and fall short of the glory of God." Every person is born into sin, and no one can measure up to God's perfect standard. This verse eliminates any illusion that we can earn our way to heaven or live a life good enough to merit God's favor. We must first acknowledge our sinful state, our inability to save ourselves.

STEP 2: THE CONSEQUENCE—ROMANS 6:23

Sin comes with a dire consequence: "For the wages of sin is death." Sin leads to spiritual death, a separation from God. But this verse doesn't end with despair; it presents hope: "But the gracious gift of God is eternal life in Christ Jesus our Lord." While our sin earns us death, God's grace offers us eternal life through Jesus. This gift is not something we can achieve; it's something we receive.

STEP 3: GOD'S DEMONSTRATION OF LOVE—ROMANS 5:8

God didn't wait for us to clean up our act. Romans 5:8 declares, "But God demonstrates His own love toward us, in that while we were still sinners, Christ died for us." Jesus' sacrificial death on the cross is the ultimate expression of God's love. He took our place, bore our punishment, and made a way for us to be reconciled with God.

STEP 4: OUR RESPONSE—ROMANS 10:9-10

Salvation requires a personal response: "If you confess with your mouth Jesus as Lord, and believe in your heart that God raised Him from the dead, you will be saved." This verse outlines the simplicity and depth of faith. It's not just intellectual assent; it's a heart-deep belief that transforms your life. Confessing Jesus as Lord means surrendering to His authority and trusting in His resurrection as the cornerstone of your faith.

STEP 5: ASSURANCE OF SALVATION—ROMANS 10:13

The journey concludes with a promise: "For everyone who calls on the name of the Lord will be saved." This is the assurance we have in Christ—no one who sincerely seeks Him will be turned away. God's offer of salvation is open to all, regardless of background, past sins, or present circumstances.

REFLECTION:

As you reflect on these verses, consider where you are in your journey of life. Have you acknowledged your need for salvation? Have you received God's gift of eternal life? If you've already walked this road, take the time to thank God today for your salvation.

Ask Him, who in your life needs to hear the Gospel of Christ? The Roman Road is not just a path to personal salvation; it's a guide we can share with others who are seeking the truth. Just pass this message along to them.

If today, you realize your need to be saved and can believe with all your heart that Jesus died for your sins and God raised Him from the dead then we invite you to say, from the heart, this prayer. A simple prayer does not save you. You must believe with your heart. The prayer is simply a way of confessing that belief in the Lord Jesus to God.

PRAYER:

Heavenly Father, I know I have sinned and come short of what you expect of me. I know I need salvation. Today, I confess Christ as my Lord. I believe Jesus died for my sins and rose from the grave. According to your holy Word, if I confess with my mouth and believe with my heart in Christ Jesus then I am saved. I thank you for saving me and I ask you to lead me now and help me live the life you have called me to. In Jesus Name, Amen.

If you prayed this prayer with all your heart and then according to God's Word you now saved. We praise God for your salvation.

Please, drop us a message at info@jehovahjirehministries.com and let us know of your decision. May God bless you as you begin "Revelation Unveiled " daily devotional.

WEEK 1: THE REVELATION OF JESUS CHRIST

Day 1: Introduction to Revelation

Day 2: The Vision of the Son of Man

Day 3: The Alpha and the Omega

Day 4: The Seven Golden Lampstands

Day 5: The One Who Holds the Keys

Day 6: The Mystery of the Seven Stars

Day 7: Living in the Revelation of Christ

DAY 1: INTRODUCTION TO REVELATION

Read Scripture: Revelation 1:1-3
Focus Scripture: Revelation 1:1 (NASB)
"The Revelation of Jesus Christ, which God gave Him to show to His bond-servants, the things which must soon take place; and He sent and communicated it by His angel to His bond-servant John."

ANECDOTE:

Picture receiving a message straight from a king, sealed with his authority and meant just for you. This is exactly what the book of Revelation represents—a direct message from the King of Kings, Jesus Christ. But this isn't just any message; it is the revelation or "unveiling" of future events, of the things that must soon take place. Imagine the awe John must have felt when he received this vision. This wasn't a casual glimpse into the future, but a life-altering, divinely orchestrated vision of what was to come, given directly by Jesus Christ, through an angel, to his loyal servant John.

EXPLANATION:

The word "revelation" comes from the Greek word *apokalupsis*, meaning "unveiling" or "disclosure." It's a fitting description for this book because it pulls back the curtain on God's future plans for humanity. Unlike many other books in the Bible, Revelation focuses on what is yet to come—events that will take place in heaven and on earth, bringing the culmination of God's redemptive plan.

The opening verse makes it clear that this revelation isn't just from John's imagination. It's the revelation of Jesus Christ, showing His bond-servants (believers) what must happen. This isn't optional information but a necessary unveiling of future events that will affect every believer. And what's more? There's a sense of urgency—these things "must soon take place," emphasizing the importance of readiness and awareness.

John was chosen to be the one to receive and record this vision while exiled on the island of Patmos. Imagine the gravity of the situation: John, the last surviving apostle, is tasked with revealing God's ultimate plan for humanity's future.

APPLICATION:

So, what does this mean for us as believers? First, Revelation is not a mystery book meant to scare or confuse us. Instead, it's an invitation to see and understand God's ultimate plan for the world. It unveils the person of Jesus Christ in His glory and shows us what lies ahead. By studying Revelation, we're not only gaining insight into future events but deepening our relationship with Jesus Christ.

Furthermore, Revelation 1:3 offers a blessing to those who read, hear, and obey the words of this prophecy. We are encouraged not just to read passively but to take its message to heart and live in light of what we learn. Jesus Himself is revealed in these pages, and as we understand more about Him, our hope in His return should grow stronger.

We also learn that the time is near. We may not know the exact day or hour of Christ's return, but the message of Revelation reminds us that we should live with an expectant heart, prepared for His second coming. How does the reality of Christ's imminent return impact your daily life? Are you living as though the King could come at any moment?

FURTHER READING:

Daniel 2:28-29, Matthew 24:30, 1 Thessalonians 5:1-2

PRAYER:

Lord Jesus, thank You for revealing Yourself through the book of Revelation. Help me to approach this study with reverence and expectation, understanding that You have a plan for the future and for my life.

Let this revelation equip me to live in anticipation of Your return and give me the courage to live faithfully for You each day. Amen.

CHALLENGE:

Reflect on how Christ's return impacts your life. Write down one area where you want to live with more intentionality, knowing that His coming is near. Ask God to help you live with a heart prepared for His return.

DAY 2: THE VISION OF THE SON OF MAN

Read Scripture: Revelation 1:4-8
Focus Scripture: Revelation 1:7 (NASB)
*"Behold, He is coming with the clouds, and every eye will
see Him, even those who pierced Him; and all the tribes of
the earth will mourn over Him. So it is to be. Amen."*

ANECDOTE:

There's something powerful about witnessing a long-awaited arrival. Whether it's a loved one returning home after years apart or watching a dignitary's grand entrance, the anticipation and excitement can be overwhelming. Now imagine a moment even greater than that—a moment when the entire world witnesses the return of Jesus Christ in glory. Revelation 1:7 paints this dramatic picture, a moment when the skies will break open, and every eye will behold the risen Savior returning to earth.

EXPLANATION:

This verse tells us that Christ will return "with the clouds," an image often associated with divine glory and majesty. His coming will not be hidden or private; it will be visible to every person on earth. This includes not just those who believe in Him but also those "who pierced Him"—those who rejected Him or had a hand in His crucifixion. This event will bring both rejoicing and mourning. For believers, Christ's return is a moment of triumph and fulfillment. But for others, it will be a time of mourning as they realize they've rejected the Savior and missed their chance to follow Him.

The scope of this event is staggering: "all the tribes of the earth" will see Him. No one will be left out. His return will be the ultimate revelation of His power and glory, and it will mark the beginning of the final chapter of human history.

APPLICATION:

How does this vision of Christ's return shape our lives today? First, it reminds us that His return is certain and that every person will one day stand face-to-face with Him. This should fill us with hope and anticipation, knowing that the Savior we trust is coming back to make all things new. But it should also stir within us a sense of urgency. Many people around us do not know Christ, and when He returns, it will be too late for them to turn to Him.

Are we living with a sense of urgency and expectation? Does the reality of Christ's return impact how we spend our time, how we treat others, and how we share the gospel? The promise of His coming should motivate us to live with purpose, making the most of every opportunity to point others to Jesus.

FURTHER READING:

Matthew 24:30, Zechariah 12:10, 1 Thessalonians 4:16-17

PRAYER:

Lord, help me to live in anticipation of Your return. Let the reality of Your coming fill me with hope and urgency to share Your love with others. Give me boldness to live faithfully in light of this promise and to point others to You, so they too may rejoice when You return. Amen.

CHALLENGE:

Identify one person in your life who doesn't know Christ. Pray for an opportunity this week to share the hope of His return with them.

DAY 3: THE ALPHA AND THE OMEGA

Read Scripture: Revelation 1:9-11
Focus Scripture: Revelation 1:11 (NASB)
"Write in a book what you see, and send it to the seven churches:
to Ephesus, and to Smyrna, and to Pergamum, and to Thyat-
ira, and to Sardis, and to Philadelphia, and to Laodicea."

ANECDOTE:

Imagine receiving a personal message from the Creator of the universe, a message so important that you are commanded to share it with others. John, while exiled on the island of Patmos, experienced this firsthand. He heard the voice of Jesus Christ instructing him to write down everything he saw and send it to the seven churches. This message wasn't just for John's benefit but for all believers—both then and now.

EXPLANATION:

In this passage, we are introduced to the seven churches of Asia Minor, which represent real churches of that time but also symbolize the universal church throughout history. The number seven in the Bible often represents completeness, suggesting that this message is for the entire church. Jesus, who calls Himself the "Alpha and Omega" (v. 8), the beginning and the end, is about to reveal truths that span the entirety of human history and eternity.

John's role here is that of a messenger. He is instructed to faithfully record and share what he sees, because these visions are not for him alone—they are for all who follow Christ. The message to the seven churches contains both encouragement and correction, and it is a call for all believers to examine their faith and remain steadfast in their commitment to Christ.

APPLICATION:

What does it mean for us today that Jesus is the Alpha and the Omega? It means that He is sovereign over all things, from the beginning of time to the end. Nothing surprises Him, and nothing is beyond His control. This should give us great comfort, knowing that our lives are in the hands of the One who holds all of history.

It also challenges us to remain faithful. Just as the churches in John's time needed to hear both encouragement and correction, we too must be open to the Holy Spirit's work in our lives. Are there areas where we've grown complacent or where we need to renew our commitment to Christ? Jesus sees the beginning and the end, and He calls us to be faithful in the present.

FURTHER READING:

Isaiah 44:6, Revelation 22:13, Colossians 1:17

PRAYER:

Lord, You are the Alpha and the Omega, the beginning and the end. Thank You for holding all of history in Your hands, including my life. Help me to trust in Your sovereignty and to remain faithful to You, no matter the circumstances. Examine my heart and show me where I need to grow in my commitment to You. Amen.

CHALLENGE:

Take time this week to reflect on your faith. Are there areas where you've grown complacent? Ask God to reveal where you need to recommit to Him and take a step of faith to renew that commitment.

DAY 4: THE SEVEN GOLDEN LAMPSTANDS

Read Scripture: Revelation 1:12-16
Focus Scripture: Revelation 1:12 (NASB)
*"Then I turned to see the voice that was speaking with me.
And having turned, I saw seven golden lampstands."*

ANECDOTE:

Think of a dark room. When you walk in, it's hard to navigate, and everything feels hidden. But once you turn on a lamp, the entire space is illuminated. You can see clearly, and what was once obscured becomes visible. In John's vision, he turns to see the voice speaking to him, and what he sees are seven golden lampstands. These lampstands represent the seven churches, shining light in the midst of a dark world.

EXPLANATION:

The lampstands symbolize the churches' role as beacons of light in a dark world. Each church has been placed strategically by Christ to shine His light, and He walks among them, ensuring their flame continues to burn. The golden lampstands signify both the value and the purpose of the church—it is precious to Christ and has a crucial mission in the world.

In the midst of this vision stands Christ Himself, described with symbolic imagery of majesty and power. His presence among the lampstands shows that He is actively involved with His church, guiding, sustaining, and evaluating each one. This is a powerful reminder that the church is not left to its own devices; Christ is deeply connected to its mission and health.

APPLICATION:

As believers, we are part of the church, the body of Christ, and we are called to shine His light in a world that is full of darkness. But how brightly is your light shining? Are you reflecting the love, truth, and grace of Christ to those around you, or has your light begun to dim?

It's easy to get distracted by the busyness of life or discouraged by the challenges we face, but this vision reminds us that Jesus is with us. He is present in His church, and He is empowering us to continue shining His light. We must remain close to Him, allowing His presence to fuel our mission.

FURTHER READING:

Matthew 5:14-16, John 8:12, Philippians 2:15

PRAYER:

Jesus, You are the light of the world, and You have called us to reflect Your light. Help me to shine brightly for You, even in the midst of darkness. Thank You for walking among Your church, sustaining and guiding us. Keep me close to You so that my light doesn't fade but continues to grow stronger each day. Amen.

CHALLENGE:

Think about how you are currently shining the light of Christ. Is there an area in your life where your light has dimmed? Ask Jesus to rekindle the flame and show you how you can shine more brightly for Him.

DAY 5: THE ONE WHO HOLDS THE KEYS

Read Scripture: Revelation 1:17-18
Focus Scripture: Revelation 1:18 (NASB)
"I am the Living One; and I was dead, and behold, I am alive forevermore, and I have the keys of death and of Hades."

ANECDOTE:

Imagine standing before a locked door with no idea how to open it. The door represents something you desperately want to enter, but without the key, it's impossible. Now, picture someone approaching, holding the very key that unlocks the door, offering it to you. Suddenly, everything changes—you have access to what was once out of reach. In Revelation 1:18, Jesus declares that He holds the keys to death and Hades, giving Him full authority over life, death, and eternity.

EXPLANATION:

The imagery of keys in the Bible often represents authority and control. In ancient times, holding the keys to a city gate or a house meant that you were in charge. You could allow access or deny it. Jesus' statement that He holds "the keys of death and Hades" is a powerful declaration of His sovereignty over life and death. As the "Living One," He conquered death through His resurrection, and now He has full authority over it. This means that for believers, death is no longer something to fear. Christ has unlocked the door to eternal life, and He alone has the power to determine our eternal destiny.

This verse also speaks of Jesus' triumph over Hades, the realm of the dead. The fact that He holds the keys to this place means that He has the ultimate say over life after death. No longer does death have dominion over us. Through His resurrection, Jesus offers us life eternal, and He holds the power to release us from the fear of death.

APPLICATION:

This truth changes everything for us as believers. The One who holds the keys to death is the same One who loves us and gave His life for us. Death is no longer a hopeless end but a doorway to eternity with Christ. How does this impact the way we live? It gives us confidence and peace, knowing that our future is secure in Him.

It also calls us to live with a sense of purpose. If Jesus has conquered death and holds the keys to eternity, how should that shape our daily lives? Are we living with boldness, knowing that death has no hold over us? Are we sharing this hope with others, knowing that Christ offers eternal life to all who trust in Him?

FURTHER READING:

Isaiah 22:22, 1 Corinthians 15:54-57, John 11:25-26

PRAYER:

Lord Jesus thank You for conquering death and holding the keys to life and eternity. Because of Your victory I no longer have to fear death. Help me live in the confidence of this truth, trusting in Your power and sharing the hope of eternal life with those around me. Amen.

CHALLENGE:

Take a moment today to reflect on any fears you have about death or the future. Surrender those fears to Christ, knowing that He holds the keys to life and death, and ask Him to fill you with peace and purpose.

DAY 6: THE MYSTERY OF THE SEVEN STARS

Read Scripture: Revelation 1:19-20
Focus Scripture: Revelation 1:20 (NASB)
"As for the mystery of the seven stars which you saw in My right hand, and the seven golden lampstands: the seven stars are the angels of the seven churches, and the seven lampstands are the seven churches."

ANECDOTE:

We all love solving mysteries. Whether it's reading a good mystery novel or figuring out a puzzle, there's something satisfying about uncovering hidden truths. In Revelation 1:20, Jesus unveils a mystery for John—the meaning behind the seven stars and the seven golden lampstands. What was hidden is now revealed: the stars represent the angels (or messengers) of the seven churches, and the lampstands represent the churches themselves. This explanation opens the door to understanding the deeper significance of John's vision.

EXPLANATION:

The seven stars symbolize the angels or messengers of the seven churches. Some scholars believe these "angels" may refer to actual angelic beings assigned to each church, while others interpret them as the pastors or leaders of the churches. Either way, the message is clear: Christ is actively involved in the life of His church. The seven lampstands, representing the churches, emphasize that each congregation has a vital role in shining the light of Christ to the world.

Jesus holds the seven stars in His right hand, a position of authority and care, showing that He has control over the church's leaders and destiny. He walks among the lampstands, demonstrating His presence with the churches. This powerful imagery reminds us that the church is precious to Jesus, and He is deeply involved in its mission and health.

APPLICATION:

Knowing that Christ holds the church and its leaders in His hand should give us comfort. The church is not just a human institution; it is the body of Christ, and He is in control. As part of His church, we have the privilege and responsibility of being a light in the world. But we are not alone. Jesus is with us, guiding and empowering His church to fulfill its mission.

In your own life, how are you contributing to the mission of the church? Are you shining brightly as part of the body of Christ, or have distractions dimmed your light? Jesus' presence with His church should inspire us to remain faithful and committed to the calling He has given us.

FURTHER READING:

Ephesians 1:22-23, Matthew 16:18, 1 Peter 2:9

PRAYER:

Jesus, thank You for holding Your church in Your hands. Help me to trust in Your leadership and care, knowing that You are present with us as we shine Your light in the world. Give me the strength to be faithful to the mission You have given me and the wisdom to follow Your leading. Amen.

CHALLENGE:

Consider how you can contribute to the mission of your local church. Whether through serving, encouraging others, or sharing the gospel, take action this week to shine the light of Christ more brightly.

DAY 7: LIVING IN THE REVELATION OF CHRIST

Read Scripture: Reflect on Revelation 1
Focus Scripture: Revelation 1:3 (NASB)
"Blessed is he who reads and those who hear the
words of the prophecy, and heed the things which
are written in it; for the time is near."

ANECDOTE:

Everyone wants to live a blessed life, but what does that really look like? In Revelation 1:3, we're given a specific promise of blessing for those who read, hear, and heed the words of this prophecy. This isn't just a general blessing for understanding future events, but a call to action—living in light of the truths we learn from Revelation. The time is near, and the message of this book is not just for the distant future but for how we live today.

EXPLANATION:

The blessing mentioned in Revelation 1:3 is unique. It's a promise directly connected to the act of engaging with this prophetic book. However, it's not just about reading or listening; the real blessing comes from "heeding," obeying what is written. This calls for an active response to the truths revealed in Revelation. The book's purpose is not merely to inform us about future events but to transform the way we live in the present.

Jesus is revealed throughout this book in His glory, majesty, and authority. His return is near, and this reality should affect how we live. The nearness of His return isn't meant to create fear but to inspire us to live with urgency, purpose, and faithfulness. The challenge is not just to know the content of Revelation but to let it shape our lives, our decisions, and our priorities.

APPLICATION:

As we reflect on the first chapter of Revelation, the question we must ask ourselves is: How will I live differently in light of what I've learned? The blessing of this book is tied to how we respond. Will we live with a greater awareness of Christ's return? Will we let His revelation stir our hearts to love and serve Him more fully?

Living in the revelation of Christ means living with hope, expectation, and a desire to reflect His glory in our everyday lives. It's not about waiting passively for His return but actively engaging in the work He's called us to, knowing that the time is near.

FURTHER READING:

James 1:22, 2 Peter 3:10-12, Matthew 7:24-27

PRAYER:

Lord, thank You for the blessing of Your Word and for revealing Your plans to us. Help me not only to hear and read the words of this prophecy but to live in obedience to them. As I wait for Your return, give me the strength to live with purpose and urgency, sharing Your love with those around me. Amen.

CHALLENGE:

Take time this week to consider how you can live in light of Christ's return. Write down one practical step you can take to align your life with the truth you've learned in Revelation 1.

WEEK 1: "INTRODUCTION TO REVELATION AND THE VISION OF CHRIST"

BEYOND THE UNVEILING: GOING DEEPER

- How does the promise of blessing in Revelation 1:3 encourage you to engage with this book of prophecy?

- Reflect on John's vision of the glorified Christ (Rev. 1:12-18). What attributes of Jesus stand out, and how do they impact your view of Him?

- What does it mean to "heed" the words of Revelation? How can you practically apply this call to heed in your daily life?

- How does the imminent return of Christ challenge you to live differently today?

- In what ways can you grow in your understanding of prophecy, and why is this important?

- How can the knowledge of Jesus' victory over death and His authority (Rev. 1:18) give you hope in difficult situations?

- What one step will you take this week to live in greater expectation of Christ's return?

WEEK 2: THE LETTERS TO THE SEVEN CHURCHES (PART 1)

DAY 1: THE CHURCH AT EPHESUS
(REV. 2:1-7)

DAY 2: THE CHURCH AT SMYRNA
(REV. 2:8-11)

DAY 3: THE CHURCH AT PERGAMUM
(REV. 2:12-17)

DAY 4: THE CHURCH AT THYATIRA
(REV. 2:18-29)

DAY 5: LESSONS FROM THE
EARLY CHURCHES

DAY 6: THE RELEVANCE OF THE
LETTERS FOR TODAY

DAY 7: PERSONAL REFLECTION:
EXAMINING MY HEART

DAY 1: A CALL TO LOVE – THE CHURCH IN EPHESUS

Read Scripture: Revelation 2:1-7
Focus Scripture: Revelation 2:4 (NASB)
"But I have this against you, that you have left your first love."

ANECDOTE:

Imagine a couple celebrating their 20th wedding anniversary. They reflect on the passion and excitement they shared when they first fell in love—the long conversations, the thoughtful gestures, the joy of simply being together. Over time, however, the busyness of life, work, and routine began to dull that initial spark. Though they still care for each other, something vital has been lost.

The church in Ephesus found itself in a similar situation. They were diligent in their work, discerning in their teaching, and persevering in their faith. But there was something missing: their first love for Jesus. Despite all their outward dedication, their hearts had grown cold, and they had forgotten the passionate devotion they once had for their Savior.

EXPLANATION:

The message to the church in Ephesus begins with words of commendation. Jesus acknowledges their hard work, perseverance, and commitment to sound doctrine. They had not tolerated false teaching and had labored faithfully for the cause of Christ. Yet despite all these positives, Jesus had one serious charge against them: they had left their first love.

Their "first love" refers to the passionate, wholehearted devotion they once had for Jesus. It's easy for churches and believers to fall into the trap of religious duty, becoming more focused on doing things for God than on loving God Himself. The Ephesian church had become so busy with the work of ministry that they had lost the vibrant, loving relationship that should have been at the center of it all. Jesus calls them to remember where they had fallen from, repent, and return to the love they once had.

APPLICATION:

This message to Ephesus speaks directly to us today. It's possible to be active in church, serve diligently, and even defend the truth, yet miss the most important thing—our love for Jesus. Is your relationship with Christ defined by passionate love or simply by duty and obligation? Have you, like the Ephesians, become so busy with "doing" that you've neglected "being" with Jesus?

If your love for Jesus has grown cold, it's not too late to return. Jesus calls us, just as He called the Ephesians, to remember the love we had at first, repent of our distracted hearts, and rekindle our devotion to Him. He desires not just our service but our hearts.

FURTHER READING:

1 Corinthians 13:1-3, Matthew 22:37-40, John 14:21

PRAYER:

Lord Jesus, forgive me for the times when I have allowed my love for You to grow cold. Help me to return to my first love, to remember the joy and passion of knowing You. May my relationship with You be more than just duty—let it be a vibrant, loving connection that drives all that I do. Amen.

CHALLENGE:

This week, take time to reflect on your relationship with Christ. Write down one step you can take to rekindle your love for Him, whether it's spending more time in prayer, meditating on His Word, or simply worshipping Him with a renewed heart.

DAY 2: FAITHFUL IN PERSECUTION – THE CHURCH IN SMYRNA

Read Scripture: Revelation 2:8-11
Focus Scripture: Revelation 2:10 (NASB)
"Do not fear what you are about to suffer. Behold, the devil is about to cast some of you into prison, so that you will be tested, and you will have tribulation for ten days. Be faithful until death, and I will give you the crown of life."

ANECDOTE:

Consider someone training for a marathon. They know the path ahead will be difficult, filled with moments of exhaustion and pain, but they push forward because they understand the reward at the end—the satisfaction of finishing the race. As believers, we are often called to endure challenges, and for the church in Smyrna, that challenge was persecution. Yet, Jesus encouraged them to be faithful, even in the face of suffering, because He had a reward waiting for them: the crown of life.

EXPLANATION:

Smyrna was a city known for its wealth, but the Christians there faced intense persecution and poverty because of their faith. They were surrounded by a culture that rejected and oppressed them, and Jesus' message to them wasn't a promise of immediate relief but an encouragement to remain faithful in the midst of suffering. Jesus tells them, "Do not fear what you are about to suffer," acknowledging the trials that lay ahead.

The reference to "ten days" of tribulation may symbolize a specific period of persecution, but the key message is not about the duration of suffering but the call to remain faithful through it. Jesus doesn't sugarcoat the reality of their situation (some would be imprisoned and tested) but He promises that their faithfulness will be rewarded with the "crown of life." This crown isn't a symbol of earthly victory but the gift of eternal life given to those who endure.

Jesus' words, "Be faithful until death," remind us that true faith is not just about enduring small inconveniences but standing firm even when our lives are at stake. His promise is clear: eternal life and victory over the "second death" (spiritual death) await those who remain faithful.

APPLICATION:

The message to the church in Smyrna is both sobering and encouraging. It reminds us that following Christ may come at a cost. While many of us may not face the same kind of persecution as the Smyrna believers, we are still called to stand firm in our faith, even when it's difficult or costly. In a world where faith can be mocked or misunderstood, Jesus' call to "be faithful until death" challenges us to remain steadfast, knowing that our hope is in eternity, not in the temporary comforts of this world.

How do you respond to trials and challenges in your faith? Do you find yourself tempted to give up or compromise when things get hard? Jesus' message encourages us to hold on, no matter what. His reward, the crown of life, is far greater than any earthly trial we may face.

FURTHER READING:

James 1:12, Matthew 5:10-12, 2 Timothy 4:7-8

PRAYER:

Lord Jesus, thank You for the promise of eternal life. Help me to remain faithful in the face of trials and challenges, trusting in Your strength to carry me through. When I am tempted to fear or give up, remind me of the crown of life that You have promised to those who endure. Give me the courage to stand firm in my faith, no matter what. Amen.

CHALLENGE:

Reflect on a time when you faced a challenge to your faith. How did you respond? Take time today to pray for believers around the world who are experiencing persecution, asking God to strengthen their faith as they endure trials.

DAY 3: HOLDING TO THE TRUTH – THE CHURCH IN PERGAMUM

Read Scripture: Revelation 2:12-17
Focus Scripture: Revelation 2:13 (NASB)
*"I know where you dwell, where Satan's throne is; and
you hold fast My name, and did not deny My faith even
in the days of Antipas, My witness, My faithful one,
who was killed among you, where Satan dwells."*

ANECDOTE:

Imagine living in a city known for its opposition to your faith. You constantly face pressure to compromise or conform, and the people around you mock what you believe. Yet, you refuse to let go of your convictions, even as the cost increases. This was the reality for the church in Pergamum, a city described as the place of "Satan's throne." Despite the spiritual and cultural challenges they faced, the believers in Pergamum held fast to the name of Jesus, even when it meant risking their lives.

EXPLANATION:

Pergamum was a city steeped in idol worship and political allegiance to Rome. It was known for its temples to Greek gods, including the famous altar to Zeus (which some believe is what Jesus meant by referring to "Satan's throne." The spiritual climate in Pergamum was hostile toward Christians, and the pressure to conform was immense. Yet, despite this environment, the believers in Pergamum remained faithful to Christ, even in the face of martyrdom. Jesus specifically commends them for holding fast to His name and not denying the faith, even when one of their own, Antipas, was killed for his testimony.

However, Jesus also had a concern for the church in Pergamum. While they had remained steadfast in some areas, they had allowed false teachings to infiltrate their midst. Some in the church followed the teachings of Balaam, which led to idolatry and immorality. The reference to Balaam is symbolic of compromise: just as Balaam led Israel into sin, these teachings were leading the church into spiritual compromise. Jesus calls them to repent and turn away from these false doctrines before it leads them further astray.

APPLICATION:

The message to Pergamum is a reminder of the importance of standing firm in the truth, even when surrounded by opposition. It also warns us about the dangers of compromise. In our world today, the pressure to conform to society's values can be overwhelming, and like the believers in Pergamum, we are often tempted to blend in or adopt beliefs that contradict Scripture.

Are there areas in your life where you've allowed compromise to creep in? It may not always be obvious, but small concessions can gradually lead us away from the truth. Jesus calls us to hold fast to His name and His Word, even when the world around us demands otherwise. But He also calls us to examine our hearts and repent when we've strayed.

FURTHER READING:

Numbers 22:1-24:25 (the story of Balaam), 1 Timothy 6:20-21, 1 Peter 5:8-9

PRAYER:

Lord Jesus, thank You for being my firm foundation in a world that often opposes Your truth. Help me to hold fast to Your name and resist the pressures to compromise. If there are areas in my life where I've allowed false beliefs or practices to enter, help me to see them and give me the courage to repent. Strengthen me to stand firm in Your truth, no matter the cost. Amen.

CHALLENGE:

This week, take some time to reflect on areas where you may be tempted to compromise your faith. Is there a particular belief or action that doesn't align with Scripture? Ask the Holy Spirit to reveal any areas of spiritual compromise and take a step toward repentance and obedience.

DAY 4: TOLERATING JEZEBEL – THE CHURCH IN THYATIRA

Read Scripture: Revelation 2:18-29
Focus Scripture: Revelation 2:20 (NASB)
"But I have this against you, that you tolerate the wom-
an Jezebel, who calls herself a prophetess, and she teach-
es and leads My bond-servants astray so that they commit
acts of immorality and eat things sacrificed to idols."

ANECDOTE:

Imagine a trusted leader in your community who begins to slowly introduce teachings and behaviors that go against the core values everyone once agreed upon. At first, people ignore or dismiss the concerns, thinking it's not a big deal. But over time, more people start to adopt these harmful practices, until the whole community is at risk of losing its identity. This was the situation in Thyatira, where false teaching had crept into the church, leading believers astray.

EXPLANATION:

Thyatira was a city known for its trade guilds, and being part of these guilds often meant participating in pagan feasts and idol worship. This created a significant challenge for the Christians in Thyatira. The church was commended for its love, faith, and service, but Jesus had a strong warning for them: they were tolerating false teaching.

A woman described as "Jezebel" (likely a symbolic reference to the evil queen found in the books of Kings in the Old Testament) was leading believers astray. She claimed to be a prophetess but taught that it was acceptable for God's people to engage in sexual immorality and eat food sacrificed to idols, which were common practices in pagan worship. Jezebel's influence was corrupting the church, much like the original Jezebel led Israel into idolatry and immorality.

Jesus called the church to account for tolerating this false teacher. While the church had many positive attributes, their failure to address the serious sin in their midst was a grave issue. Jesus warned them that unless they repented, judgment would come, not only on Jezebel but also on those who followed her teachings.

APPLICATION:

The church in Thyatira had many strengths, but their tolerance of sin was leading them down a dangerous path. This message reminds us that while love and service are essential in the Christian life, we must also stand firm in truth. There's a difference between loving others and tolerating sin that leads to spiritual destruction.

Are there areas in your life where you've tolerated sinful behaviors or beliefs, perhaps out of a desire to avoid conflict or maintain peace? It can be tempting to overlook sin, but Jesus calls us to confront it with grace and truth. He doesn't tolerate sin, and neither should we. While we are called to love others, we must also uphold the purity of the church and our lives.

Jesus promises that those who overcome will share in His authority and reign with Him. He encourages the faithful in Thyatira not to give in to the false teachings but to hold fast to the truth.

FURTHER READING:

1 Kings 16:29-33 (the story of Queen Jezebel), 1 Corinthians 5:6-7, Matthew 18:15-17

PRAYER:

Lord Jesus, thank You for Your love and mercy, but also for Your call to purity and truth. Help me to stand firm in Your Word and not tolerate sin in my life or the lives of those around me. Give me the courage to lovingly confront what is wrong, and the wisdom to walk in Your truth. Amen.

CHALLENGE:

Reflect on areas where you may have tolerated sin in your own life or in the lives of others. Pray for the courage to address it with grace and truth, and ask God to help you uphold His standards of purity in all areas of life.

DAY 5: STRENGTHEN WHAT REMAINS – THE CHURCH IN SARDIS

Read Scripture: Revelation 3:1-6
Focus Scripture: Revelation 3:2 (NASB)
"Wake up, and strengthen the things that remain, which were about to die; for I have not found your deeds completed in the sight of My God."

ANECDOTE:

Have you ever seen a plant that looks healthy on the outside but is slowly withering away at its roots? At first glance, it might seem fine, but with time, the symptoms of decay become visible. Without immediate action, it will soon die. The church in Sardis was much like that plant—outwardly they appeared alive, but Jesus saw that their faith was dying from within. He called them to wake up and strengthen what was left before it was too late.

EXPLANATION:

Sardis was a city that had a reputation for wealth and prestige. The church in Sardis seemed to reflect this on the surface—they had a reputation for being alive, but in reality, they were spiritually dead. Jesus' rebuke was direct: "I know your deeds, that you have a name that you are alive, but you are dead." This was a church that was going through the motions, maintaining an appearance of life and vitality, but their hearts were far from God.

Jesus' warning was urgent. The spiritual life that remained in Sardis was fading fast, and they needed to act immediately to strengthen what little was left. Their works were incomplete before God, meaning they were not living up to their calling as followers of Christ. Jesus tells them to "wake up" and "remember what you have received and heard," calling them to return to the truth of the gospel and live out their faith with sincerity.

Yet, even in the midst of this sobering message, there is hope. Jesus acknowledges that there is still a faithful remnant, those who have not "soiled their garments" and who walk faithfully with Him. For those who overcome, Jesus promises they will walk with Him in white garments, a symbol of purity and victory, and their names will remain in the Book of Life.

APPLICATION:

The message to Sardis is a wake-up call for all believers. It's easy to get caught up in outward appearances, doing good deeds, attending church, and maintaining a religious routine, while neglecting the true condition of our hearts. Jesus sees beyond our actions and reputation—He looks at the state of our spiritual life.

Are there areas in your faith that are withering, even if everything seems fine on the surface? Perhaps you've allowed your relationship with Christ to grow stagnant, or maybe you're relying on past experiences rather than seeking fresh encounters with Him. Jesus calls us to wake up, return to Him, and strengthen what remains before it fades away.

This passage also reminds us of the importance of perseverance. Those who remain faithful, even when others grow spiritually complacent, will be rewarded with eternal life and the promise that their names will not be blotted out of the Book of Life.

FURTHER READING:

James 2:14-17, Matthew 23:25-28, Hebrews 10:22-25

PRAYER:

Lord Jesus, wake me up from any spiritual slumber I may be in. Help me to strengthen the areas of my life that are weak and return to the passion and commitment I once had for You. Thank You for Your grace and for the promise of life to those who remain faithful. Keep me close to You and help me live out my faith with sincerity and purpose. Amen.

CHALLENGE:

Examine your spiritual life honestly. Are there areas where your faith has grown weak or stagnant? Write down one action you can take to strengthen your relationship with Christ, whether it's renewing your time in prayer, seeking fellowship, or studying His Word with fresh eyes.

DAY 6: THE OPEN DOOR – THE CHURCH IN PHILADELPHIA

Read Scripture: Revelation 3:7-13
Focus Scripture: Revelation 3:8 (NASB)
"I know your deeds. Behold, I have put before you an open door which no one can shut, because you have a little power, and have kept My word, and have not denied My name."

ANECDOTE:

Think of a time when an unexpected opportunity presented itself—maybe it was a new job, a chance to make a difference in someone's life, or a fresh start after a period of struggle. The excitement of stepping through that "open door" can bring hope and purpose, knowing that it's a chance to move forward in a new direction. For the church in Philadelphia, Jesus set an open door before them, representing a unique opportunity to advance His kingdom, despite their small strength.

EXPLANATION:

The church in Philadelphia was not large or powerful, but they were faithful. Jesus acknowledged that they had "a little power," meaning that they were not influential in worldly terms, but they had kept His word and remained loyal to His name. In response to their faithfulness, Jesus placed an open door before them, a door that represented opportunities for ministry, evangelism, and kingdom work that no one could shut.

Unlike some of the other churches in Revelation, Jesus had no words of rebuke for Philadelphia. He commended them for their perseverance and loyalty in the face of opposition. This church, though small and perhaps overlooked by the world, was spiritually strong because of their unwavering commitment to Christ.

Jesus promised that those who opposed them—symbolized by the "synagogue of Satan"—would eventually acknowledge the truth and that

Philadelphia's faithful members would be protected from the coming "hour of testing" that would come upon the world. Furthermore, Jesus promises that those who overcome will be made pillars in the temple of God, a symbol of permanence and honor in His eternal kingdom.

APPLICATION:

The message to the church in Philadelphia is a powerful reminder that faithfulness matters more than worldly influence or strength. Jesus doesn't require us to be powerful, wealthy, or prominent, He simply calls us to be faithful with what we've been given. Even when we feel weak or insignificant, He can open doors of opportunity that no one can shut.

Is there an open door in your life right now? It may be an opportunity to serve, share the gospel, or make a difference in the lives of those around you. Jesus has placed this open door before you, and He asks that you step through it in faith. Even if you feel like you only have "a little power," your faithfulness is what matters to Him.

Additionally, the promise of being a "pillar in the temple of God" reminds us that our faithfulness now will lead to eternal rewards. Jesus calls us to remain steadfast in our commitment to Him, knowing that He is preparing a place for us in His eternal kingdom.

FURTHER READING:

1 Corinthians 16:9, Colossians 4:3, Matthew 25:23

PRAYER:

Lord Jesus, thank You for opening doors in my life that no one can shut. Help me to step through them with faith, even when I feel weak or inadequate. Thank You for valuing my faithfulness, and help me to remain committed to You, trusting in Your strength and provision. May I walk in obedience and trust You with the opportunities You place before me. Amen.

CHALLENGE:

Take time this week to reflect on any "open doors" in your life. Whether it's a new opportunity or a chance to serve, pray for the courage and faith to step through those doors. Trust that God will provide the strength you need, even if you feel you have little power.

DAY 7: LUKEWARM FAITH – THE CHURCH IN LAODICEA

Read Scripture: Revelation 3:14-22
Focus Scripture: Revelation 3:16 (NASB)
*"So because you are lukewarm, and neither hot
nor cold, I will spit you out of My mouth."*

ANECDOTE:

Imagine taking a sip of water expecting it to be refreshing (either cool and crisp or warm and soothing) but instead, it's tepid and unappealing. You might instinctively spit it out because it's neither hot nor cold, neither refreshing nor comforting. In the same way, Jesus uses the image of lukewarm water to describe the spiritual condition of the church in Laodicea—a faith that had become stale and ineffective.

EXPLANATION:

Laodicea was a wealthy city known for its industry and self-sufficiency, but spiritually, the church was in a dangerous place. Jesus' strongest rebuke in the letters to the seven churches is directed at Laodicea. The believers there had become spiritually lukewarm, neither hot with passion for Christ nor cold with outright rejection. Instead, they were comfortable, complacent, and indifferent, living as if they had no need for anything, not even God.

Laodicea's lukewarmness stemmed from their reliance on their material wealth. They believed they were "rich" and in need of nothing, but Jesus tells them they are spiritually "wretched, miserable, poor, blind, and naked." Their self-sufficiency had blinded them to their true spiritual condition. Jesus urges them to "buy from Me gold refined by fire," symbolizing genuine faith, and to clothe themselves in white garments, representing righteousness. He also invites them to receive spiritual sight through the "eye salve" that only He can provide.

Despite His rebuke, Jesus' words are filled with love. He tells them, "Those whom I love, I reprove and discipline." Jesus wasn't condemning them out of anger but out of a desire to restore them to a place of spiritual vitality. He stands at the door of their hearts, knocking, ready to come in and renew their relationship if they will repent and invite Him in.

APPLICATION:

The message to Laodicea challenges us to examine our own spiritual temperature. Have we become lukewarm in our faith? It's easy to slip into complacency when life is comfortable, but Jesus calls us to be passionate and wholehearted in our devotion to Him. Lukewarm faith is neither refreshing to the world nor pleasing to God.

Jesus offers the solution: return to Him, acknowledge our need for Him, and allow Him to reignite our hearts. He invites us to open the door and let Him in, promising deep fellowship and intimacy with those who respond.

Is your faith marked by passion and love for Christ, or has it grown lukewarm? Jesus longs to rekindle the fire in your heart and restore you to a place of spiritual vitality.

FURTHER READING:

James 1:22-25, Romans 12:11, 2 Timothy 1:6-7

PRAYER:

Lord Jesus, forgive me for the times when I have grown lukewarm in my faith. Help me to recognize my need for You in every area of my life. Rekindle the fire of passion for You in my heart and let me live with wholehearted devotion to You. Thank You for Your loving correction, and for standing at the door, ready to come in and renew our relationship. Amen.

CHALLENGE:

Evaluate your spiritual temperature. If there are areas where your faith has become lukewarm, ask Jesus to reignite your passion for Him. Make a plan to spend intentional time in prayer, worship, and reading His Word this week, seeking to deepen your relationship with Him.

WEEK 2: "THE LETTERS TO THE SEVEN CHURCHES (PART 1)"

BEYOND THE UNVEILING, GOING DEEPER

- Which message to the churches resonates most with you, and why?

- How does Jesus' call for repentance apply to your life today?

- Reflect on the promises Jesus makes to those who overcome (Rev. 2-3). Which promise speaks most deeply to you?

- What challenges or temptations might be causing you to lose focus on your "first love"?

- How can the struggles of the early churches inspire your walk with Christ?

- How would you describe the health of your spiritual life based on Jesus' assessment of the churches?

- How can you practically support and pray for your local church this week?

Dr. Ralph W. Jenkins

WEEK 3: MESSAGES TO THE SEVEN CHURCHES (PART 2)

Day 1: The Church's First Love Restored – Ephesus

Day 2: Remaining Faithful in Persecution – Smyrna

Day 3: Conquering Compromise – Pergamum

Day 4: Rejecting False Teaching – Thyatira

Day 5: Reviving Spiritual Life – Sardis

Day 6: Strengthening Through Perseverance – Philadelphia

Day 7: Overcoming Lukewarmness – Laodicea

DAY 1: THE CHURCH'S FIRST LOVE RESTORED – EPHESUS

Read Scripture: Revelation 2:1-7
Focus Scripture: Revelation 2:5 (NASB)
"Therefore remember from where you have fallen, and repent and do the deeds you did at first; or else I am coming to you and will remove your lampstand out of its place—unless you repent."

ANECDOTE:

Think back to when you first fell in love with something: a new hobby, a passion, or even a person. The excitement and dedication you felt were unwavering. But over time, distractions and the pressures of life might have dulled that initial passion. In Revelation 2:1-7, the church of Ephesus had lost the passion for Christ they once had. While they were diligent in their work and doctrine, Jesus saw the heart issue: they had abandoned their first love.

EXPLANATION:

Jesus begins by commending the Ephesian believers for their hard work, perseverance, and commitment to the truth. They had stood against false teaching and refused to tolerate evil. However, He had one significant charge against them: they had lost their first love. Their love for Jesus, which should have been the core of their faith, had cooled.

This passage offers both a warning and a solution. Jesus calls them to "remember from where you have fallen," urging them to reflect on their former love and passion. Next He tells them to repent and return to the works they did at first, implying that their faith had become more about duty than genuine love. If they failed to do so, Jesus warned He would remove their lampstand, which meant losing their effectiveness as a church.

APPLICATION:

This message to Ephesus reminds us that our relationship with Jesus is not just about doing things for Him, but about loving Him. Have you allowed the busyness of life or the work of ministry to overshadow your personal relationship with Christ? Like the Ephesians, we may be doing all the right things outwardly, but Jesus is more concerned with the condition of our hearts. He calls us to return to our first love and rekindle our passion for Him.

Spend time today reflecting on your love for Jesus. Are you motivated by love, or have you become caught up in routine? Jesus invites us to repent and return to the passion we once had for Him. When we do, we restore the joy and intimacy of our relationship with Christ.

FURTHER READING:

Matthew 22:37-40, John 14:15, 1 Corinthians 13:1-3

PRAYER:

Lord Jesus, forgive me for the times I have allowed my love for You to grow cold. Help me to remember the passion I once had for You and restore that love in my heart. May my relationship with You be the foundation of everything I do, and let me serve You with joy and devotion. Amen.

CHALLENGE:

Take time this week to reflect on your relationship with Christ. Write down one way you can rekindle your love for Him, whether it's spending more time in prayer, worship, or Scripture.

DAY 2: REMAINING FAITHFUL IN PERSECUTION – SMYRNA

Read Scripture: Revelation 2:8-11
Focus Scripture: Revelation 2:10 (NASB)
"Do not fear what you are about to suffer. Behold, the devil is about to cast some of you into prison, so that you will be tested, and you will have tribulation for ten days. Be faithful until death, and I will give you the crown of life."

ANECDOTE:

Imagine someone training for a marathon. They know the race ahead will be long and challenging, but they continue pushing forward, knowing that the reward at the finish line makes the struggle worthwhile. The church in Smyrna faced a much greater challenge than physical endurance, they faced persecution. Yet, Jesus encouraged them to remain faithful, promising them the "crown of life" if they endured.

EXPLANATION:

Smyrna was a city known for its wealth, but the Christians there faced poverty and persecution because of their faith. Jesus' message to them wasn't a promise of relief from suffering, but an encouragement to endure it. He acknowledges the trials they are about to face, including imprisonment and testing, but tells them not to fear. He promises that their suffering will be limited (symbolized by the "ten days"), and that if they remain faithful, they will receive the crown of life, eternal life with Him.

Jesus commends them for their faithfulness, even though they were physically poor and oppressed by those who falsely claimed to be believers. He reminds them that true wealth lies in their spiritual riches. His command is simple but profound: "Be faithful until death." This faithfulness, even in the face of martyrdom, would lead to the greatest reward of all.

APPLICATION:

The message to Smyrna reminds us that following Jesus may come at a cost. While we may not face the same level of persecution, we are still called to be faithful in the face of trials. How do you respond when your faith is tested? Do you stand firm, or do you waver when things get hard?

Jesus calls us to be faithful, even when life is difficult, and promises that our faithfulness will be rewarded. The crown of life is not just a symbol of eternal life but a reminder that Christ has already won the victory. No matter what trials we face, we can trust in Him and the reward that awaits us in eternity.

FURTHER READING:

James 1:12, Matthew 5:10-12, 2 Timothy 4:7-8

PRAYER:

Lord Jesus, thank You for the promise of eternal life. Help me to remain faithful, even when my faith is tested. When I am tempted to give up or give in to fear, remind me of the crown of life You have promised. Strengthen me to stand firm in my faith, no matter the cost. Amen.

CHALLENGE:

Take some time this week to pray for believers who are facing persecution around the world. Ask God to strengthen their faith and grant them courage as they endure trials for His name.

DAY 3: CONQUERING COMPROMISE – PERGAMUM

Read Scripture: Revelation 2:12-17
Focus Scripture: Revelation 2:14 (NASB)
"But I have a few things against you, because you have there some who hold the teaching of Balaam, who kept teaching Balak to put a stumbling block before the sons of Israel, to eat things sacrificed to idols and to commit acts of immorality."

ANECDOTE:

Imagine working hard to maintain a healthy lifestyle, exercising and eating well. But over time, small compromises—an extra dessert here, skipping a workout there—begin to undermine your progress. Slowly, without realizing it, you fall into unhealthy patterns. In a similar way, the church in Pergamum was faithful in many ways, but they had allowed subtle compromises to take root, which threatened to derail their spiritual health.

EXPLANATION:

Pergamum was a city with deep ties to idolatry and emperor worship. The church there had remained faithful to Christ in many ways, even in the face of persecution. However, they had allowed compromise to slip into their community. Some in the church were following the "teaching of Balaam," a reference to the Old Testament story where Balaam led Israel into idolatry and sexual immorality (Numbers 25). This compromise involved tolerating pagan practices, such as eating food sacrificed to idols and participating in immoral activities.

Jesus' rebuke is clear: while the church had done well in some areas, they were allowing sin to go unchecked. He called them to repentance, warning that if they didn't deal with these compromises, He would come and fight against them with the "sword of His mouth," symbolizing the authority of His Word.

Despite this warning, Jesus also offers a promise. Those who overcome will receive "hidden manna," symbolizing spiritual nourishment, and a "white stone" with a new name, a sign of victory, approval, and a unique relationship with Christ.

APPLICATION:

The message to Pergamum is a reminder that compromise can be subtle, but it is dangerous. It's easy to let small concessions to sin slip into our lives, thinking they won't have much impact. But over time, those compromises can lead us away from the truth. Jesus calls us to remain faithful and pure in our devotion to Him, not allowing the values of the world to infiltrate our hearts.

Are there areas in your life where you've compromised? Perhaps it's in your morals, relationships, or the entertainment you consume. Jesus calls us to repent and return to Him, dealing with compromise before it takes root. He offers the promise of spiritual nourishment and victory to those who remain faithful.

FURTHER READING:

Numbers 25:1-3, 1 Corinthians 10:21-22, James 4:4

PRAYER:

Lord Jesus, thank You for the truth of Your Word that guides me. Help me to recognize areas of compromise in my life and give me the strength to turn away from them. Let me remain faithful to You, not allowing the values of the world to influence my heart. Thank You for the promise of victory and spiritual nourishment when I remain true to You. Amen.

CHALLENGE:

Examine your life for any areas of compromise. Ask the Holy Spirit to reveal where you may have allowed sin to slip in, and take a step toward repentance and purity today.

DAY 4: REJECTING FALSE TEACHING – THYATIRA

Read Scripture: Revelation 2:18-29
Focus Scripture: Revelation 2:20 (NASB)
"But I have this against you, that you tolerate the woman Jezebel, who calls herself a prophetess, and she teaches and leads My bond-servants astray so that they commit acts of immorality and eat things sacrificed to idols."

ANECDOTE:

Think of someone you trust deeply, someone whose advice you value. Now imagine if that person started leading you down the wrong path, telling you things that sound good but are ultimately harmful. That's what happened to the church in Thyatira. They were strong in many ways, but they had tolerated false teaching, allowing themselves to be led astray.

EXPLANATION:

The church in Thyatira was known for its love, faith, service, and perseverance. Jesus acknowledges these strengths, but He has a serious charge against them: they were tolerating a false teacher, symbolically referred to as "Jezebel," who was leading believers into idolatry and sexual immorality.

The name "Jezebel" refers back to the wicked queen in the Old Testament who led Israel into idol worship and immorality. In Thyatira, this "Jezebel" claimed to be a prophetess and was teaching that it was acceptable for Christians to engage in practices associated with idol worship, including acts of immorality.

Jesus' rebuke is strong. He warns that those who follow this false teaching will face judgment if they do not repent. Yet, even in His warning, Jesus offers hope: those who repent will be spared, and those who remain faithful will be rewarded with authority and the "morning star," a symbol of Christ Himself.

APPLICATION:

This message calls us to be vigilant against false teaching. In today's world, there are many voices that claim to speak truth but lead people away from the heart of the gospel. Whether it's teachings that distort Scripture or cultural values that contradict God's Word, we must be discerning in what we allow into our lives and into our churches.

Are you vigilant in guarding against false teaching? Are you allowing the truth of Scripture to guide your decisions and beliefs, or have you let outside influences shape your thinking? Jesus calls us to reject anything that leads us away from Him and to hold fast to His Word.

FURTHER READING:

1 Kings 16:29-33, 1 Timothy 6:3-5, 2 Peter 2:1-3

PRAYER:

Lord Jesus, protect me from false teaching and anything that would lead me away from You. Give me discernment to recognize truth from error, and the courage to reject anything that contradicts Your Word. Help me hold fast to Your truth and remain faithful to You. Amen.

CHALLENGE:

Evaluate the teachings you follow and the influences in your life. Are they leading you closer to Christ or away from Him? Take steps to remove anything that doesn't align with God's Word and seek out truth.

DAY 5: REVIVING SPIRITUAL LIFE – SARDIS

Read Scripture: Revelation 3:1-6
Focus Scripture: Revelation 3:2 (NASB)
"Wake up, and strengthen the things that remain, which were about to die; for I have not found your deeds completed in the sight of My God."

ANECDOTE:

Imagine a fire that has been burning brightly but now is reduced to glowing embers. There's still heat, but without attention, it will soon die out. This was the spiritual condition of the church in Sardis. They had once been alive in their faith, but now they were barely holding on. Jesus called them to wake up and fan the flames before their faith was completely extinguished.

EXPLANATION:

Sardis had a reputation for being alive, but Jesus saw the truth: they were spiritually dead. While they may have looked active and vibrant from the outside, their works were incomplete, and their faith was withering away. Jesus' message to them was urgent: they needed to wake up and strengthen what little remained before it died completely.

The command to "wake up" implies that the believers in Sardis had become complacent and spiritually lazy. They were going through the motions without real devotion to Christ. Jesus called them to remember the truth they had once received, to repent, and to complete the work they had left unfinished.

Yet, even in Sardis, there was a remnant of faithful believers. Jesus promised that those who overcome will be clothed in white garments, symbolizing purity and victory, and that their names would never be erased from the Book of Life.

APPLICATION:

The message to Sardis is a wake-up call for all of us. It's easy to fall into a spiritual slumber, going through the motions of faith without real passion or commitment. But Jesus calls us to examine our hearts, repent where needed, and strengthen what remains of our faith before it fades away.

Are you spiritually alive, or have you allowed your faith to wither? Jesus offers the chance for renewal and revival if we will turn to Him and allow Him to reignite the flame in our hearts.

FURTHER READING:

Matthew 25:1-13, 2 Timothy 1:6, Romans 13:11

PRAYER:

Lord Jesus, wake me up from any spiritual slumber I may be in. Help me to strengthen the areas of my faith that are weak and revive my passion for You. Thank You for Your grace and for calling me to a deeper, more vibrant relationship with You. Amen.

CHALLENGE:

Examine your spiritual life honestly. Are there areas where your faith has grown weak or stagnant? Write down one action you can take to strengthen your relationship with Christ, whether through prayer, fellowship, or studying His Word.

DAY 6: STRENGTHENING THROUGH PERSEVERANCE – PHILADELPHIA

Read Scripture: Revelation 3:7-13
Focus Scripture: Revelation 3:8 (NASB)
"I know your deeds. Behold, I have put before you an open door which no one can shut, because you have a little power, and have kept My word, and have not denied My name."

ANECDOTE:

Imagine being part of a small team, facing enormous challenges, yet knowing that someone much greater than you has your back. No matter how difficult the circumstances, you're not alone, and the opportunities before you are assured. The church in Philadelphia was small and faced opposition, yet Jesus had opened a door for them that no one could close. Their strength lay not in numbers or power but in their faithfulness to Christ.

EXPLANATION:

Philadelphia was a city known for its strategic location and opportunities for outreach. The believers there, though small and seemingly weak, were commended by Jesus for their faithfulness. He recognized that they had "a little power," meaning they were not influential by worldly standards, yet they had remained faithful to His word and had not denied His name, even in the face of pressure and opposition.

Jesus' promise to this church was profound: He had set before them an "open door" that no one could shut. This door likely symbolized opportunities for ministry and the advancement of the gospel. Though they were weak in human terms, Christ Himself was empowering them to carry out His mission.

Additionally, Jesus promised that those who were opposing them—the "synagogue of Satan"—would eventually recognize the truth and acknowledge that Jesus had loved them. Jesus also assured the believers in

Philadelphia that He would keep them from the "hour of testing" that was to come upon the world, perhaps a reference to protection during trials or the ultimate deliverance in the end times.

APPLICATION:

The message to Philadelphia is encouraging for anyone who feels weak or inadequate. Jesus doesn't require us to have great strength or influence; He asks for faithfulness. Even when we feel small or overlooked, God can open doors of opportunity for us that no one can shut. He honors those who remain true to His Word and continue to follow Him, regardless of the challenges.

Are you feeling weak or discouraged in your faith? Do you wonder if your efforts are making a difference? Jesus sees your faithfulness, and promises that He is the one who opens doors and sustains you through trials. Take heart and know that your faithfulness matters to Him, and He is preparing a reward for those who endure.

FURTHER READING:

Colossians 4:3, Isaiah 22:22, 1 Corinthians 16:9

PRAYER:

Lord Jesus, thank You for the open doors You place before me, even when I feel weak. Help me to remain faithful to Your Word and trust that You will guide and strengthen me. Give me the perseverance to continue following You, knowing that my strength comes from You alone. Amen.

CHALLENGE:

Consider the "open doors" in your life—opportunities for service, evangelism, or growth. Ask God to help you walk through those doors with faith, even if you feel you have "little power." Trust in His strength to guide you through.

DAY 7: OVERCOMING LUKEWARMNESS – LAODICEA

Read Scripture: Revelation 3:14-22
Focus Scripture: Revelation 3:16 (NASB)
"So because you are lukewarm, and neither hot nor cold, I will spit you out of My mouth."

ANECDOTE:

Imagine taking a sip of water that you expect to be either refreshingly cold or soothingly warm, only to find that it's tepid and unappealing. You might instinctively want to spit it out because it offers no real satisfaction. This is how Jesus describes the spiritual condition of the church in Laodicea: neither passionate nor rejecting, but lukewarm, and therefore distasteful to Him.

EXPLANATION:

Laodicea was a wealthy city, known for its commerce and self-sufficiency, but the church there had become complacent. Jesus' strongest rebuke among the seven churches is directed at Laodicea. He describes them as "lukewarm." They were comfortable, self-reliant, and indifferent, thinking they needed nothing, not even God.

Jesus' assessment is sharp: though they believed themselves to be "rich," they were actually "wretched, miserable, poor, blind, and naked" in a spiritual sense. Their wealth and self-sufficiency had blinded them to their true spiritual poverty. Jesus urged them to "buy from Me gold refined by fire," symbolizing true faith, and to "clothe" themselves in white garments, representing righteousness.

Despite His rebuke, Jesus offers an invitation: "Behold, I stand at the door and knock." He is ready to restore their relationship with Him if they will repent and invite Him back into the center of their lives. For those who overcome, Jesus promises a place with Him on His throne, a position of honor and authority.

APPLICATION:

The message to Laodicea challenges us to evaluate our own spiritual condition. Have we become lukewarm in our faith? It's easy to become comfortable, relying on our own resources or routines, but Jesus calls us to passionate, wholehearted devotion. Lukewarmness is not pleasing to Him, and He calls us to repent and return to a vibrant, intimate relationship with Him.

Jesus doesn't want half-hearted followers. He invites us to a deeper, more fulfilling relationship with Him, where He becomes the center of our lives. Are you spiritually lukewarm, or is your faith marked by passion and love for Christ? He stands at the door, ready to come in and restore what has been lost.

FURTHER READING:

James 1:22-25, Romans 12:11, 2 Timothy 1:6-7

PRAYER:

Lord Jesus, forgive me for the times when I have grown lukewarm in my faith. Help me to recognize my need for You in every area of my life and reignite my passion for You. Thank You for standing at the door, ready to restore our relationship. Let me live with wholehearted devotion to You. Amen.

CHALLENGE:

Evaluate your spiritual "temperature." If there are areas where your faith has become lukewarm, ask Jesus to reignite your passion for Him. Commit to spending intentional time in prayer, worship, and seeking His presence this week.

WEEK 3: "MESSAGES TO THE SEVEN CHURCHES (PART 2)"

BEYOND THE UNVEILING, GOING DEEPER

- How does the message to Laodicea challenge you to assess your own "spiritual temperature"?

- In what ways can you ensure that you're "holding fast" in your faith, like the church in Philadelphia?

- What are some practical ways to combat spiritual complacency in your life?

- How does Jesus' promise to the faithful in Philadelphia encourage you?

- Reflect on any areas of compromise you may have allowed in your life. What steps can you take to address these?

- How does understanding the warnings given to the churches impact your sense of urgency in following Christ?

- What specific steps will you take this week to strengthen your faith and commitment?

WEEK 4: THE BLESSED HOPE – ENCOURAGEMENT THROUGH THE RAPTURE

Day 1: The Door Standing Open – Revelation 4:1

Day 2: Caught Up Together – 1 Thessalonians 4:13-14

Day 3: Comfort One Another – 1 Thessalonians 4:15-18

Day 4: Behold, I Am Coming Quickly – Revelation 4:2-3

Day 5: Escape from Wrath – Revelation 4:4-6

Day 6: Before the Throne – Revelation 4:9-10

Day 7: Encourage and Watch – Titus 2:11-13

DAY 1: THE DOOR STANDING OPEN

Read Scripture: Revelation 4:1
Focus Scripture: Revelation 4:1 (NASB)
*"After these things I looked, and behold, a door standing open
in heaven, and the first voice which I had heard, like the sound
of a trumpet speaking with me, said, 'Come up here, and I
will show you what must take place after these things.'"*

ANECDOTE:

Imagine being invited to step through a door that leads to another world—a place where everything is transformed, where you can see clearly what lies ahead. In Revelation 4:1, the apostle John is invited into such a place, a heavenly vision of the future. This "open door" represents not only John's vision but also the moment when believers will be called up to meet the Lord. It's a powerful picture of the rapture, the moment when the church is caught up into heaven.

EXPLANATION:

The language of Revelation 4:1 is striking. John hears a voice like a trumpet saying, "Come up here," and suddenly he is taken into the heavenly throne room. Many pretribulation scholars view this verse as symbolic of the rapture of the church, that moment when believers will be caught up to meet the Lord in the air before the tribulation begins.

The "open door" signifies an invitation, not only for John but for the entire body of believers, to enter into the presence of God. The "trumpet" echoes the language of 1 Thessalonians 4:16, where the trumpet of God sounds to call the dead in Christ and those who are alive to be caught up together with the Lord.

This event is a source of great hope and encouragement for believers. The rapture will take place before the judgments of the tribulation, reminding us that as followers of Christ, we are not appointed to suffer the wrath of God. Instead, we will be taken into His presence, to experience the glory of heaven and the fulfillment of His promises.

APPLICATION:

The open door in Revelation 4:1 is a reminder of the blessed hope we have in Christ. As we look forward to the rapture, we can live in confidence that Jesus will take us to be with Him before the tribulation begins. This gives us comfort and motivation to live faithfully, knowing that our future is secure.

Are you living with the anticipation of Christ's return? The promise of the rapture should inspire us to live with urgency, knowing that Jesus could come at any moment. As we wait for that open door, let's remain steadfast in our faith and share the good news with others, so they too can have the hope of being caught up with Christ.

FURTHER READING:

1 Corinthians 15:51-52, John 14:2-3, Matthew 24:42-44

PRAYER:

Lord, thank You for the promise of the rapture and the open door into Your presence. Help me to live with a heart that is ready and waiting for Your return. Give me the courage to share this hope with others, and may my life reflect the joy and anticipation of being with You forever. Amen.

CHALLENGE:

Take time today to reflect on the hope of the rapture. Are there areas in your life where you need to live with greater urgency and expectation of Christ's return? Write down one practical step you can take to prepare your heart for that open door.

DAY 2: CAUGHT UP TOGETHER

Read Scripture: 1 Thessalonians 4:13-14
Focus Scripture: 1 Thessalonians 4:14 (NASB)
"For if we believe that Jesus died and rose again, even so God will bring with Him those who have fallen asleep in Jesus."

ANECDOTE:

Imagine being separated from a loved one, only to be reunited after a long absence. The joy and relief of that moment are indescribable. In the same way, Paul describes the reunion of believers with Christ at the rapture, an event that will bring together those who have died in Christ and those who are alive at His coming. It's a powerful moment of reunion, comfort, and joy.

EXPLANATION:

In 1 Thessalonians 4:13-14, Paul addresses the concern of believers in Thessalonica who were grieving the death of fellow Christians. They wondered what would happen to those who had "fallen asleep" (a term Paul uses for death) when Christ returned. Paul offers words of hope and assurance: just as Jesus died and rose again, so too will God bring with Him those who have died in Christ.

This passage is foundational for understanding the rapture. Paul explains that when Jesus returns, the dead in Christ will rise first, and then those who are alive will be caught up together with them in the clouds to meet the Lord in the air (v. 16-17). This moment of being "caught up" is the rapture—a joyful reunion with Jesus and with all believers, both living and dead.

For Christians, the rapture is not something to fear but something to look forward to with great anticipation. It's the fulfillment of God's promise to bring His people into His presence, and it's a reminder that death is not the end for those who are in Christ.

APPLICATION:

The promise of being "caught up together" with Christ should bring us comfort in times of grief and loss. Knowing that death is not the final word for believers, we can face the future with hope. The rapture is not just about escaping the tribulation, it's about being united with Christ and with our fellow believers in eternal joy.

Is there someone you are grieving today? Let the hope of the rapture and the resurrection bring you peace, knowing that in Christ, we will be reunited with those who have gone before us. This hope should also motivate us to live in such a way that we are ready for Christ's return, faithfully following Him until that day.

FURTHER READING:

1 Corinthians 15:50-58, John 11:25-26, Philippians 3:20-21

PRAYER:

Lord Jesus, thank You for the promise that we will be caught up together with You and with all believers who have gone before us. Help me to live in the hope of the resurrection and to comfort others with the assurance of eternal life. May my life reflect the joy of knowing that death has no power over those who belong to You. Amen.

CHALLENGE:

Reach out to someone who may be grieving the loss of a loved one and share with them the hope of the rapture and the resurrection. Let them know that in Christ, death is not the end but the beginning of eternal life.

DAY 3: COMFORT ONE ANOTHER

Read Scripture: 1 Thessalonians 4:15-18
Focus Scripture: 1 Thessalonians 4:18 (NASB)
"Therefore comfort one another with these words."

ANECDOTE:

Think of a time when you received news that brought you deep comfort, perhaps in the midst of uncertainty or grief. The right words at the right time can bring peace to a troubled heart. In 1 Thessalonians 4:15-18, Paul gives believers words of ultimate comfort: Jesus is coming back, and we will be united with Him forever. No matter what we face, this truth is a source of encouragement and hope.

EXPLANATION:

In this passage, Paul gives more detail about the rapture. He explains that when Jesus returns, the dead in Christ will rise first, and those who are alive will be caught up with them to meet the Lord in the air. This is not just a momentary event; it's the beginning of our eternal life in the presence of Jesus. Paul's instruction to the Thessalonians is clear: "Comfort one another with these words."

Why does Paul emphasize comfort? Because the reality of the rapture provides assurance that we do not need to fear death or the future. For believers, the rapture is not something to dread but something to anticipate with joy. It's a promise that we will be with the Lord forever, and that nothing—no trial, no suffering, no tribulation—can separate us from His love.

This is the foundation of our hope: that no matter what happens in this life, we have an eternal future with Jesus. Paul's message to the Thessalonians was meant to lift their spirits and to give them peace, knowing that Christ's return was certain and their future was secure.

APPLICATION:

These words of comfort are just as powerful today as they were for the Thessalonian church. In a world filled with uncertainty, fear, and loss, the promise of Christ's return and the rapture provides us with an anchor of hope. We can face the challenges of this life with confidence, knowing that Jesus is coming back for us.

Are you living with the comfort of the rapture in mind? Let this promise bring peace to your heart in times of difficulty. And just as Paul encouraged the Thessalonians, we are called to comfort one another with this truth. Who in your life needs to hear these words of hope? Share the comfort of the rapture with those around you, reminding them that Jesus is coming back for His church.

FURTHER READING:

Romans 8:38-39, John 14:1-3, 2 Corinthians 1:3-4

PRAYER:

Lord, thank You for the comfort of Your return and the promise of the rapture. Help me to live each day in the hope of this truth, and give me the words to comfort others who may be struggling. May I find peace in knowing that I will be with You forever, and let this assurance bring comfort to those around me. Amen.

CHALLENGE:

Take a moment today to encourage someone who is going through a difficult time with the hope of Christ's return. Share with them the comfort of knowing that Jesus will come back for His people, and that we will be with Him forever.

DAY 4: BEHOLD, I AM COMING QUICKLY

Read Scripture: Revelation 4:2-3
Focus Scripture: Revelation 22:12 (NASB)
*"Behold, I am coming quickly, and My reward is with Me,
to render to every man according to what he has done."*

ANECDOTE:

When you know a special event is coming soon (a wedding, a vacation, or a visit from a loved one) you prepare for it with eager anticipation. Every detail matters because the arrival of that moment brings excitement and joy. In the same way, Jesus tells us, "Behold, I am coming quickly." The return of Christ is not a distant event but one that could happen at any moment, and it should fill our hearts with anticipation and readiness.

EXPLANATION:

In Revelation 4:2-3, John is immediately "in the Spirit" and transported into the heavenly throne room, where he sees a vision of God's majesty. This swift transition into heaven is a reminder of the suddenness of Christ's return. Throughout the book of Revelation, Jesus frequently says, "Behold, I am coming quickly," emphasizing the imminence of His return.

For believers, the rapture represents the fulfillment of this promise. While we do not know the day or the hour, we are called to live in readiness, knowing that Jesus could return at any moment. His return will be both a time of reward for those who have faithfully followed Him and a time of fulfillment for all of God's promises.

The phrase "I am coming quickly" is not meant to induce fear, but to encourage us to stay spiritually alert and focused on what truly matters. We are called to live with eternity in view, knowing that everything we do should be in preparation for that moment when we will meet the Lord face-to-face.

APPLICATION:

The knowledge that Jesus is coming quickly should inspire us to live lives of purpose and readiness. Are you living with the expectation that Christ could return at any moment? Or have you become distracted by the busyness and concerns of this world?

Take time today to refocus on what matters most. Let the promise of Christ's soon return fill your heart with anticipation and joy. And as you live in light of this truth, make sure you are sharing the good news with those around you, so that they too can be ready for His coming.

FURTHER READING:

Matthew 24:36-44, Revelation 22:7, 1 John 2:28

PRAYER:

Lord Jesus, thank You for the promise that You are coming quickly. Help me to live in a state of readiness, anticipating Your return with joy and excitement. Let my life reflect the urgency of the gospel, and give me the courage to share Your truth with those who need to hear it. Amen.

CHALLENGE:

Reflect on how you can live more purposefully in light of Christ's return. What areas of your life need to be realigned with this truth? Take one step today to live with greater spiritual readiness.

DAY 5: ESCAPE FROM WRATH

Read Scripture: Revelation 4:4-6
Focus Scripture: 1 Thessalonians 1:10 (NASB)
"And to wait for His Son from heaven, whom He raised from the dead, that is Jesus, who rescues us from the wrath to come."

ANECDOTE:

Imagine being warned of a coming storm—a hurricane or a tornado—knowing that safety is available, but only for those who act on the warning. For believers, the rapture represents an escape from the "storm" of God's wrath that will come during the tribulation. Through Jesus, we are promised rescue from this time of judgment, and we can take comfort in knowing that God has made a way for us to be saved.

EXPLANATION:

In Revelation 4:4-6, John describes the heavenly throne room and the twenty-four elders seated around the throne, representing the redeemed people of God. This vision occurs before the events of the tribulation, indicating that the church is safely in heaven before the judgments of Revelation 6 begin.

The Bible clearly teaches that those who are in Christ are not appointed to suffer God's wrath. In 1 Thessalonians 1:10, Paul reminds believers that Jesus "rescues us from the wrath to come." This wrath refers to the judgments that will be poured out during the tribulation, a time of unprecedented suffering on the earth. However, those who have trusted in Christ will not experience this wrath, as they will be taken to heaven through the rapture.

This promise of rescue is a source of hope and encouragement for believers. While the world may face judgment, we are secure in Christ, knowing that He has provided a way of escape from the wrath to come.

This truth should inspire us to live with confidence and joy, even in uncertain times.

APPLICATION:

The promise of being rescued from God's wrath should bring us comfort and peace. We do not need to fear the future, because Jesus has already made a way for us to be saved. Are you living with the assurance of this truth?

Let the knowledge of Christ's rescue fill your heart with gratitude and confidence. And as you reflect on the grace you have received, think about how you can share this hope with others. Many people around us are unaware of the coming judgment, and we have the opportunity to point them to the One who can rescue them.

FURTHER READING:

Romans 5:9, 1 Thessalonians 5:9-10, Revelation 3:10

PRAYER:

Lord Jesus, thank You for rescuing me from the wrath to come. I praise You for the assurance that I am safe in Your hands, and I pray for the courage to share this hope with others. Help me to live in the confidence of Your grace, knowing that You have made a way for me to escape judgment and experience eternal life. Amen.

CHALLENGE:

Think of someone in your life who may not know about the coming judgment or the hope of Christ's rescue. Pray for an opportunity to share the gospel with them this week and point them to the promise of salvation through Jesus.

DAY 6: BEFORE THE THRONE

Read Scripture: Revelation 4:9-10
Focus Scripture: Revelation 4:10 (NASB)
"The twenty-four elders will fall down before Him who sits on the throne, and will worship Him who lives forever and ever, and will cast their crowns before the throne."

ANECDOTE:

Have you ever been in the presence of someone so important or revered that you couldn't help but show them the utmost respect? In Revelation 4:9-10 we see a glimpse of heavenly worship as the twenty-four elders fall before the throne of God, casting their crowns in a profound act of reverence and submission. This scene gives us a picture of the honor and worship that will take place in heaven, as believers stand before the throne of God.

EXPLANATION:

The twenty-four elders in Revelation represent the redeemed people of God, and their presence in heaven before the tribulation begins is a powerful reminder of the rapture's timing. They are seated on thrones, wearing crowns, which symbolize the rewards they have received for their faithfulness.

But as they worship the One who sits on the throne, they cast their crowns before Him, recognizing that all they have comes from God. Their worship is not just a matter of words, but of action, laying down their crowns in humility and surrender.

This scene reminds us of the glory that awaits believers in heaven. We will not only be in the presence of God, but we will have the privilege of worshiping Him face-to-face. The crowns we receive for our faithfulness will be cast at His feet, acknowledging that He alone is worthy of all honor and praise.

APPLICATION:

The scene of heavenly worship invites us to consider how we are living today. Are we living in such a way that our lives bring honor to God? The crowns we receive are not for our own glory but for His. We are called to live with the awareness that everything we do should point to Him.

Let the promise of standing before God's throne motivate you to live faithfully now. One day, we will stand before Him, and what a joy it will be to cast our crowns at His feet in worship. Until then, let's live with humility and surrender, honoring Him in all that we do.

FURTHER READING:

Matthew 25:21, 1 Peter 5:4, 2 Corinthians 5:10

PRAYER:

Lord, I look forward to the day when I will stand before Your throne and worship You face-to-face. Help me to live each day with the desire to bring honor and glory to Your name. May my life be marked by humility, surrender, and worship, as I seek to glorify You in all things. Amen.

CHALLENGE:

Reflect on how you are living in light of eternity. Are your actions, decisions, and words bringing honor to God? Make a commitment today to live with the awareness that one day you will stand before His throne in worship.

DAY 7: ENCOURAGE AND WATCH

Read Scripture: Titus 2:11-13
Focus Scripture: Titus 2:13 (NASB)
"Looking for the blessed hope and the appearing of the glory of our great God and Savior, Christ Jesus."

ANECDOTE:

Have you ever eagerly awaited the arrival of someone special, watching for any sign that they were about to appear? The anticipation grows as you look forward to that joyful reunion. In Titus 2:13, Paul describes the return of Christ as our "blessed hope," the event we should all be eagerly watching and waiting for with joy and excitement. This hope is not just wishful thinking, but a certain promise that Jesus is coming again.

EXPLANATION:

The "blessed hope" of the believer is the return of Christ, when He will appear in glory and take us to be with Him forever. This hope is not something distant or uncertain; it is a promise that should shape the way we live today. Paul encourages believers to live "sensibly, righteously, and godly" as we wait for this glorious event.

The return of Christ is not only a source of comfort but also a call to action. We are to live with a sense of purpose, knowing that at any moment, Jesus could come back for His church. This truth should motivate us to live lives that honor Him, to share the gospel with others, and to remain watchful and ready.

This "blessed hope" is not just about escaping the trials of this world; it's about looking forward to the glorious future that awaits us in the presence of God. Our lives should be marked by joy and anticipation, as we watch and wait for the appearing of our Savior.

APPLICATION:

Are you living in light of the "blessed hope"? The return of Christ should fill our hearts with joy and purpose, knowing that our future is secure in Him. But it should also inspire us to live with urgency, sharing the hope we have with others and preparing our hearts for His return.

Take time today to reflect on the hope of Christ's return. Let this truth bring you encouragement in difficult times, and let it motivate you to live with purpose and anticipation. We don't know the day or the hour, but we know the promise is certain: Jesus is coming back, and we will be with Him forever.

FURTHER READING:

1 Peter 1:3-5, 2 Peter 3:10-13, Matthew 24:42-44

PRAYER:

Lord Jesus, thank You for the blessed hope of Your return. Help me to live each day in anticipation of that moment, watching and waiting for Your glorious appearing. Let my life reflect the joy of knowing that my future is secure in You, and give me the courage to share this hope with others. Amen.

CHALLENGE:

Take time today to encourage someone with the hope of Christ's return. Share with them the promise of the rapture and the joy that comes from knowing we will be with the Lord forever.

WEEK 4: "THE BLESSED HOPE – ENCOURAGEMENT THROUGH THE RAPTURE"

BEYOND THE UNVEILING, GOING DEEPER

- How does the concept of the rapture influence your perspective on current events?

- Reflect on the encouragement found in knowing that Jesus will return for His church. How does this shape your daily life?

- How can you comfort others with the hope of the rapture?

- In what ways can you prepare for Christ's return, practically and spiritually?

- What aspects of the rapture bring you the greatest hope?

- How does the promise of escape from wrath deepen your understanding of God's grace?

- How can you share the hope of the rapture with someone this week?

WEEK 5: THE HEAVENLY THRONE AND THE WORSHIP OF GOD

DAY 1: THE THRONE ROOM OF HEAVEN – REVELATION 4:1-3

DAY 2: THE MAJESTY OF GOD – REVELATION 4:4-6

DAY 3: THE FOUR LIVING CREATURES – REVELATION 4:7-8

DAY 4: WORSHIP AROUND THE THRONE – REVELATION 4:9-11

DAY 5: THE SCROLL AND THE LAMB – REVELATION 5:1-4

DAY 6: WORTHY IS THE LAMB – REVELATION 5:5-7

DAY 7: ALL CREATION WORSHIPS THE LAMB – REVELATION 5:8-14

DAY 1: THE THRONE ROOM OF HEAVEN

Read Scripture: Revelation 4:1-3
Focus Scripture: Revelation 4:2 (NASB)
"Immediately I was in the Spirit; and behold, a throne was standing in heaven, and One sitting on the throne."

ANECDOTE:

Have you ever entered a room so majestic that it took your breath away? Perhaps it was an awe-inspiring cathedral, a grand palace, or a natural landscape that left you speechless. In Revelation 4, John is given a glimpse into the very throne room of heaven, and the sight is far beyond anything we can imagine on earth. This vision sets the stage for the unfolding of God's ultimate plan and reminds us of His sovereign rule over all creation.

EXPLANATION:

John's vision begins with a door standing open in heaven, inviting him to witness something extraordinary. The first thing John sees is a throne, symbolizing God's sovereign rule and authority. This throne is not empty; it is occupied by "One sitting on the throne," pointing to God's presence as the ultimate ruler of the universe.

John describes the One on the throne in terms of precious stones: jasper and sardius (or carnelian), which reflect the beauty, majesty, and holiness of God. A rainbow encircles the throne, appearing like an emerald, a reminder of God's covenant faithfulness and mercy. This scene immediately draws our attention to the majesty and glory of God, who is not distant or disconnected but reigning from His throne.

The image of the throne is central in Revelation. It is a symbol of God's ultimate authority, and everything that follows in the book of Revelation flows from this vision of God's sovereignty.

APPLICATION:

As believers, this vision of the throne room is a powerful reminder that God is in control. No matter what happens in the world or in our personal lives, God is seated on His throne, and nothing can dethrone Him. When we face challenges or uncertainties, we can take comfort in the fact that our God reigns.

Is there an area of your life where you've struggled to trust God's sovereignty? Take time today to reflect on this vision of the heavenly throne room and remind yourself that God is in control even when circumstances seem out of control.

FURTHER READING:

Psalm 103:19, Isaiah 6:1-3, Ezekiel 1:26-28

PRAYER:

Lord, thank You for the vision of Your throne room in Revelation, reminding me of Your majesty and sovereignty. Help me to trust in Your rule over my life and to rest in the assurance that You are in control, no matter what I face. May I live each day with the confidence that You are seated on the throne, reigning over all creation. Amen.

CHALLENGE:

Identify one area in your life where you struggle to trust God's authority. Surrender that area to Him today, knowing that He reigns from His throne and has the power to work all things for good.

DAY 2: THE MAJESTY OF GOD

Read Scripture: Revelation 4:4-6
Focus Scripture: Revelation 4:6 (NASB)
"And before the throne there was something like a sea of glass, like crystal; and in the center and around the throne, four living creatures full of eyes in front and behind."

ANECDOTE:

Have you ever stood at the edge of the ocean, marveling at the vastness and beauty of the water stretching endlessly before you? The ocean is often used as a symbol of majesty and mystery, its depths unfathomable. In John's vision of heaven, a "sea of glass, like crystal" is spread before God's throne, a stunning picture of His majesty, holiness, and power.

EXPLANATION:

Surrounding God's throne are 24 elders, seated on thrones, wearing white garments and golden crowns. These elders likely represent the faithful people of God—both from the Old Testament (the twelve tribes of Israel) and the New Testament (the twelve apostles). Their position on thrones signifies the honor and authority given to them by God, but their white garments and crowns reflect purity and victory.

In front of the throne is something like a "sea of glass," appearing like crystal. This vast sea represents the separation between God's holiness and creation's impurity, as well as the peace and stillness that flow from God's sovereign reign. Unlike the turbulent seas of the earth, this sea is calm and clear, symbolizing the peace that surrounds God's throne.

At the center of this scene, we see four living creatures, full of eyes, signifying their complete awareness and watchfulness. These creatures, as we will explore, play a central role in the worship of God and reflect His creative power and majesty.

APPLICATION:

The sea of glass and the majesty of God's throne remind us of His transcendence and holiness. God is not like us. He is infinitely greater, beyond anything we can fully comprehend. Yet He invites us to come near, to worship Him, and to be part of His eternal kingdom.

Do you take time to reflect on God's majesty in your daily life? In the busyness of life, it's easy to lose sight of God's holiness and greatness. Take time today to simply stand in awe of who He is and worship Him for His majesty.

FURTHER READING:

Exodus 24:10, 1 Timothy 6:15-16, Isaiah 40:28-31

PRAYER:

Lord God, I stand in awe of Your majesty and holiness. Help me to never lose sight of Your greatness, and let my heart be filled with wonder and worship as I reflect on who You are. May Your majesty and peace reign in my life, and may I live in a way that honors You as the holy, sovereign King. Amen.

CHALLENGE:

Set aside time today to worship God simply for who He is. Reflect on His majesty and holiness, and let your heart be filled with awe and reverence as you spend time in His presence.

DAY 3: THE FOUR LIVING CREATURES

Read Scripture: Revelation 4:7-8
Focus Scripture: Revelation 4:8 (NASB)

"And the four living creatures, each one of them having six wings, are full of eyes around and within; and day and night they do not cease to say, 'Holy, holy, holy is the Lord God, the Almighty, who was and who is and who is to come.'"

ANECDOTE:

In nature, we are often captivated by the diversity of living creatures, each uniquely designed, from the majesty of a soaring eagle to the strength of a lion. In Revelation 4, John witnesses a vision of four living creatures unlike anything on earth. These creatures are not only unique in appearance but play a crucial role in heaven's continual worship of God.

EXPLANATION:

The four living creatures around God's throne are described with striking imagery: one like a lion, one like a calf, one with the face of a man, and one like a flying eagle. These creatures, with six wings and eyes all around, symbolize the fullness of God's creation and His power over all living things.

Each of these creatures likely represents different aspects of God's creation: the lion symbolizes majesty and strength, the calf (or ox) represents service and power, the man reflects intelligence, and the eagle represents swiftness and sovereignty. Together, they encompass the variety and richness of life, all created to glorify God.

Day and night, these creatures never stop declaring, "Holy, holy, holy is the Lord God Almighty." Their worship is continuous, reflecting the eternal nature of God's holiness and sovereignty. As we join in their song, we are reminded that worship is not confined to a specific time or place, it is the constant response of all creation to the majesty of God.

APPLICATION:

The worship of the living creatures challenges us to consider how we view worship in our own lives. Is worship something we reserve for specific moments, or is it the continual posture of our hearts? These creatures never cease to proclaim God's holiness, and their example reminds us that worship should be the center of our lives, flowing from a deep recognition of who God is.

Do you find yourself drifting away from worship during the busyness of life? How can you cultivate a heart of continuous worship, where your thoughts, actions, and words reflect your love for God?

FURTHER READING:

Isaiah 6:1-4, Ezekiel 1:10, Colossians 1:16

PRAYER:

Holy, holy, holy are You, Lord God Almighty. Help me to live a life of continual worship, recognizing Your holiness and power in every aspect of my life. May my heart be set on praising You, not only in moments of song but in every thought, word, and action. Amen.

CHALLENGE:

Make worship a continuous part of your day. Whether through prayer, singing, or simply meditating on God's holiness, take time throughout the day to reflect on who He is and offer Him praise.

DAY 4: WORSHIP AROUND THE THRONE

Read Scripture: Revelation 4:9-11
Focus Scripture: Revelation 4:11 (NASB)
"Worthy are You, our Lord and our God, to receive glory and honor and power; for You created all things, and because of Your will they existed, and were created."

ANECDOTE:

Think about a time when you felt overwhelming gratitude and awe. Maybe it was standing before a magnificent view, witnessing a beautiful act of kindness, or reflecting on the love of someone close to you. In those moments, it's natural to express praise and thanks. In Revelation 4, we see a vision of unceasing worship as all of heaven breaks into praise around God's throne, recognizing His worthiness as Creator and King.

EXPLANATION:

John's vision of worship around the throne is one of the most awe-inspiring images in Revelation. As the living creatures continually declare God's holiness, the 24 elders fall down in worship before Him who sits on the throne. The elders cast their crowns before the throne, a symbolic act of surrender and submission, recognizing that any authority or honor they possess comes from God alone.

The worship of the elders culminates in a powerful declaration: "Worthy are You, our Lord and our God, to receive glory and honor and power." This praise is not given out of obligation but out of deep recognition of who God is: the Creator of all things. Everything that exists, exists because of God's will and for His glory. His power is unmatched, His authority absolute, and His worthiness infinite.

This scene reminds us that worship in heaven is centered on God's character and His role as Creator. It also points to the reality that our purpose, as part of His creation, is to glorify Him. We exist because of His will, and our lives are meant to reflect His glory.

APPLICATION:

The worship of the elders challenges us to reflect on the centrality of worship in our own lives. Worship is not just something we do on Sundays or in moments of song, it is a lifestyle of recognizing and declaring God's worthiness in everything we do. The act of casting their crowns before God shows the humility and surrender that true worship requires.

Are there areas in your life where you struggle to submit to God's authority? Are you holding on to your own crown of control or success, rather than laying it before Him? True worship involves not only praising God with our words but surrendering our lives to His will.

Take time today to reflect on God's worthiness and to surrender any areas of your life that you have not fully given to Him.

FURTHER READING:

1 Chronicles 16:29, Psalm 95:6-7, Romans 12:1

PRAYER:

Lord, You are worthy of all glory, honor, and power. Help me to live a life of true worship, recognizing Your authority over every part of my life. I surrender my crowns of control, success, and pride to You, knowing that everything I have comes from You. Let my life reflect Your glory in all that I do. Amen.

CHALLENGE:

Identify one area of your life where you need to submit more fully to God's authority. Take a step of surrender today, laying that "crown" before Him in worship and trust.

DAY 5: THE SCROLL AND THE LAMB

Read Scripture: Revelation 5:1-4
Focus Scripture: Revelation 5:2-3 (NASB)
"And I saw a strong angel proclaiming with a loud voice, 'Who is worthy to open the book and to break its seals?' And no one in heaven or on the earth or under the earth was able to open the book or to look into it."

ANECDOTE:

Imagine being handed a sealed letter, knowing it contains incredibly important information, but you're unable to open it. The anticipation grows as you realize no one around you can open it either. The sense of frustration and helplessness builds. This is the scene John witnesses in Revelation 5, as a scroll sealed with seven seals appears in heaven, and no one is found worthy to open it—until the Lamb steps forward.

EXPLANATION:

The scroll in this vision represents God's unfolding plan for history and the redemption of creation. It is sealed with seven seals, indicating that its contents are hidden and secure, and only someone worthy can open it. The question is proclaimed across heaven: "Who is worthy to open the scroll and break its seals?"

The weight of this moment is significant. The opening of the scroll is not just about revealing future events, but about executing God's sovereign plan of salvation and judgment. However, no one—whether angelic beings or humans—was found worthy to open the scroll. John's response is one of deep sorrow, as he begins to weep, understanding the importance of this scroll and the inability of anyone to access it.

This scene highlights humanity's limitations and the need for a worthy Redeemer. Left to ourselves, we cannot accomplish God's plan or access the fullness of His purposes. But this is not the end of the story.

APPLICATION:

John's weeping over the unopened scroll reminds us of the deep longing for redemption and restoration that exists in every heart. We all long for the world to be made right, for justice to prevail, and for God's plan to be fulfilled. But we are powerless on our own to bring this about.

This passage invites us to acknowledge our dependence on God's plan and His Redeemer. Only Jesus, the Lamb, is worthy to open the scroll and bring about the fulfillment of God's purposes. In your own life, are you trusting in your own ability to control or fix things, or are you looking to Jesus, the only one worthy to bring about God's perfect plan?

FURTHER READING:

Isaiah 29:11-12, Daniel 12:4, Hebrews 10:19-23

PRAYER:

Lord Jesus, I recognize that You alone are worthy to open the scroll and to fulfill God's plan. Help me to trust in You, knowing that only You can bring about the redemption and restoration that I long for. Let me rest in the assurance that Your plan is perfect, and help me to surrender my need for control to You. Amen.

CHALLENGE:

Reflect on areas in your life where you may be trying to take control, rather than trusting in God's plan. Surrender those areas to Him today, and rest in the knowledge that Jesus alone is worthy to fulfill His purposes.

DAY 6: WORTHY IS THE LAMB

Read Scripture: Revelation 5:5-7
Focus Scripture: Revelation 5:5 (NASB)
*"And one of the elders said to me, 'Stop weeping; behold,
the Lion that is from the tribe of Judah, the Root of David,
has overcome so as to open the book and its seven seals.'"*

ANECDOTE:

Have you ever experienced a moment of despair when it felt like all hope was lost, only to have someone step in and change everything? It's as if the situation was completely turned around, and what seemed impossible became possible. That's the scene in Revelation 5. John is weeping because no one is found worthy to open the scroll, but then the Lamb steps forward—Jesus, the Lion of Judah—who alone is worthy to fulfill God's redemptive plan.

EXPLANATION:

As John weeps over the unopened scroll, one of the elders approaches him with words of comfort and hope. He tells John to stop weeping because there is One who is worthy to open the scroll: the Lion of the tribe of Judah, the Root of David. These titles point to the messianic prophecies about Jesus, who is both the powerful Lion (representing His kingly authority) and the descendant of David (fulfilling the promise of a ruler who would reign forever).

John then sees the Lamb standing in the center of the throne. This Lamb, though appearing as though it had been slain, is alive and victorious. The image of Jesus as both the Lion and the Lamb reveals His dual nature. He is the conquering King, yet also the sacrificial Savior who was slain for the sins of the world.

The Lamb takes the scroll from the hand of the One who sits on the throne, signifying that Jesus alone is worthy to bring about the unfolding of God's redemptive plan. His victory through His death and resurrection makes Him the only one able to fulfill the destiny of humanity and creation.

APPLICATION:

The contrast between John's weeping and the appearance of the Lamb reminds us that Jesus is the answer to our deepest longings and needs. He is the only one who can bring hope where there is despair, victory where there is defeat, and redemption where there is brokenness. As the Lion of Judah, He has overcome every enemy, and as the Lamb of God, He has provided the way for us to be reconciled to God.

Do you find yourself in a place of despair or hopelessness? Remember that Jesus, the Lion and the Lamb, has already overcome. He alone is worthy to bring about God's purposes in your life. Trust in His victory and His ability to redeem even the darkest situations.

FURTHER READING:

Genesis 49:9-10, Isaiah 11:1-2, John 1:29

PRAYER:

Lord Jesus, thank You for being both the Lion of Judah and the Lamb of God. In You, I find both power and sacrifice. Help me to trust in Your victory and to surrender any areas of hopelessness or despair to You, knowing that You alone are worthy to open the scroll and fulfill God's plan. Amen.

CHALLENGE:

Reflect on any areas in your life where you feel hopeless or defeated. Bring those to Jesus, the victorious Lion and sacrificial Lamb, and trust in His power to redeem and restore.

DAY 7: ALL CREATION WORSHIPS THE LAMB

Read Scripture: Revelation 5:8-14
Focus Scripture: Revelation 5:13 (NASB)
"And every created thing which is in heaven and on the earth and under the earth and on the sea, and all things in them, I heard saying, 'To Him who sits on the throne, and to the Lamb, be blessing and honor and glory and dominion forever and ever.'"

ANECDOTE:

Have you ever been part of a crowd that erupted into joyful celebration, whether at a concert, a sporting event, or a moment of collective victory? The energy and unity of that moment can be overwhelming, as everyone joins together in one voice of praise. In Revelation 5, we see a scene of universal worship as all creation joins in praising God and the Lamb. The celebration is not for a temporary victory, but for the eternal triumph of God's plan and the worthiness of the Lamb who was slain.

EXPLANATION:

After the Lamb takes the scroll, all of heaven bursts into worship. The four living creatures and the 24 elders fall before the Lamb, holding harps and bowls of incense, which represent the prayers of the saints. They sing a new song, declaring that the Lamb is worthy to take the scroll and to open its seals because He was slain and redeemed people from every nation through His blood.

But this scene of worship doesn't stop with the heavenly beings. As John continues to watch, the worship expands to include every creature in heaven, on earth, under the earth, and in the sea. All of creation joins in declaring the worthiness of the Lamb and the One who sits on the throne. This is a picture of the ultimate purpose of creation: to glorify God and the Lamb.

The universal scope of this worship reminds us that Jesus' redemption extends beyond individuals, it encompasses all of creation. Every being, every creature, every part of the created world joins in this cosmic act of worship, proclaiming the eternal glory of God.

APPLICATION:

This passage invites us to join in the worship of the Lamb, recognizing that Jesus is worthy of all honor, glory, and praise. Worship is not just a Sunday activity; it is the natural response of all creation to the greatness of God and the salvation provided by Jesus. The worship of heaven reminds us that our lives should be marked by continual praise, as we live in light of who God is and what He has done.

Are you living a life of worship, recognizing the worthiness of the Lamb in your daily actions, thoughts, and words? This passage calls us to align our hearts with the heavenly worship we see in Revelation, giving glory to God in every aspect of our lives.

FURTHER READING:

Psalm 148:7-13, Philippians 2:9-11, Colossians 1:16-17

PRAYER:

Lord Jesus, You are worthy of all honor, glory, and praise. Help me to join with all creation in worshiping You, not just in moments of song but in every part of my life. May my actions, thoughts, and words reflect Your worthiness, and may I live in continual praise of the Lamb who was slain. Amen.

CHALLENGE:

As you go about your day, look for opportunities to worship God in the small things. Whether through a simple prayer, a kind action, or a moment of reflection, let worship flow naturally as you respond to the worthiness of the Lamb.

WEEK 5: "THE HEAVENLY THRONE AND THE WORSHIP OF GOD"

BEYOND THE UNVEILING, GOING DEEPER

- Reflect on the vision of the heavenly throne room. How does it change your understanding of God's majesty?

- How can worship bring you closer to God in times of hardship?

- What does it mean for you personally that Christ is "worthy" to receive honor and praise?

- How can you incorporate elements of worship from Revelation 4 and 5 into your daily life?

- What lessons on worship do you learn from the heavenly hosts and elders in this passage?

- Reflect on a time when worship brought you peace. How did that experience shape your relationship with God?

- In what ways can you deepen your personal and corporate worship this week?

WEEK 6: THE FOUR HORSEMEN OF THE APOCALYPSE

Day 1: The White Horse – The Conqueror (Revelation 6:1-2)

Day 2: The Red Horse – War and Bloodshed (Revelation 6:3-4)

Day 3: The Black Horse – Famine and Scarcity (Revelation 6:5-6)

Day 4: The Pale Horse – Death and Hades (Revelation 6:7-8)

Day 5: The Cry of the Martyrs (Revelation 6:9-11)

Day 6: The Great Earthquake (Revelation 6:12-14)

Day 7: The Wrath of the Lamb (Revelation 6:15-17)

DAY 1: THE WHITE HORSE – THE CONQUEROR

Read Scripture: Revelation 6:1-2
Focus Scripture: Revelation 6:2 (NASB)
*"I looked, and behold, a white horse, and he who
sat on it had a bow; and a crown was given to him,
and he went out conquering and to conquer."*

ANECDOTE:

Imagine watching a world leader rise to power, seemingly bringing peace and prosperity, yet something feels off. The promises are empty, and the peace is short-lived. This is the image we see in the rider on the white horse in Revelation 6, a figure who appears to be a conqueror, but his true intentions are deceptive. This horseman represents the beginning of the tribulation, where a false sense of peace leads to worldwide chaos.

EXPLANATION:

The first seal in Revelation reveals a rider on a white horse, symbolizing conquest. At first glance, this rider may appear similar to Christ (who also rides a white horse in Revelation 19), but the differences are clear. This rider has a bow but no arrows, signifying conquest through deception or diplomacy rather than force. He is given a crown, indicating that his authority is permitted by God, but his reign is part of the judgment on a world that has rejected the true King.

This rider represents the Antichrist, who will rise to power during the early part of the tribulation. He will bring a false sense of peace, deceiving many into following him. This peace will be short-lived. It is a prelude to the devastation that follows with the next horsemen.

APPLICATION:

The arrival of the white horse reminds us of the danger of deception. In a world that is increasingly hostile to the truth, it's easy to be led astray by leaders or movements that promise peace but deliver chaos. As believers, we must be grounded in God's Word, discerning the difference between true peace, which comes from Christ, and false peace, which the world offers.

Though this passage speaks of a future event, it serves as a reminder to hold fast to the truth and to be wary of anyone or anything that promises peace apart from Jesus. While the world may be deceived, we have the assurance that our true Conqueror is Christ, and His peace is eternal.

FURTHER READING:

1 Thessalonians 5:3, Matthew 24:4-5, 2 Thessalonians 2:9-12

PRAYER:

Lord Jesus, help me to be discerning in a world filled with deception. Strengthen my faith so that I am not led astray by false promises of peace. Thank You for being the true Conqueror, and for the peace that only You can bring. Amen.

CHALLENGE:

Reflect on areas in your life where you may be seeking peace apart from Christ. Surrender those areas to Him today, knowing that only He can bring lasting peace.

DAY 2: THE RED HORSE – WAR AND BLOODSHED

Read Scripture: Revelation 6:3-4
Focus Scripture: Revelation 6:4 (NASB)
"And another, a red horse, went out; and to him who sat on it, it was granted to take peace from the earth, and that men would slay one another; and a great sword was given to him."

ANECDOTE:

Think of a time when you witnessed conflict on a personal or global scale, whether a heated argument between friends or a report of war on the news. The pain and destruction that follow can leave deep wounds. In Revelation 6, the rider on the red horse brings war and bloodshed to the earth, taking away the peace that many had believed was secure.

EXPLANATION:

The second seal reveals a rider on a red horse, symbolizing war and bloodshed. This horseman is given the power to take peace from the earth, leading people to turn against one another in violent conflict. The peace that the first rider established is now shattered, and the true nature of the tribulation begins to unfold.

War and conflict have been present throughout human history, but during the tribulation, it will intensify in a way the world has never seen. Nations will rise against each other, and the result will be widespread violence, death, and destruction. The sword given to the rider signifies the large-scale conflict that will engulf the earth.

While this passage paints a grim picture of the future, it also reminds us that God is sovereign, even over the chaos of war. The rider is given a sword, meaning his power is permitted by God for a time, but it will not last forever.

APPLICATION:

As we read about the red horse, we are reminded of the fragile nature of peace in this world. Wars and conflicts may come, but as believers, our hope is in the Prince of Peace, Jesus Christ. Though the world will experience violence and unrest, we can rest in the assurance that God's kingdom is one of peace, and that in the end, His reign will be established.

Are you anxious about the conflicts and turmoil in the world today? Take comfort in knowing that God is in control, even in the midst of chaos. While the world may be filled with conflict, we can have peace in Christ, knowing that He will one day bring an end to all war and establish His kingdom of peace.

FURTHER READING:

Matthew 24:6-7, Isaiah 2:4, John 16:33

PRAYER:

Lord Jesus, thank You for being my peace in the midst of a troubled world. Help me to trust in Your sovereignty, even when I see conflict and war around me. Strengthen my heart, and remind me that You are in control, and that one day You will bring lasting peace. Amen.

CHALLENGE:

Pray for areas of the world or people in your life who are experiencing conflict. Ask God to bring peace, healing, and restoration, and to use you as an instrument of His peace in those situations.

DAY 3: THE BLACK HORSE – FAMINE AND SCARCITY

Read Scripture: Revelation 6:5-6
Focus Scripture: Revelation 6:6 (NASB)
"And I heard something like a voice in the center of the four living creatures saying, 'A quart of wheat for a denarius, and three quarts of barley for a denarius; and do not damage the oil and the wine.'"

ANECDOTE:

Consider a time when a natural disaster struck and resources became scarce. Prices skyrocketed, and simple necessities were suddenly difficult to find. In such moments, the fragility of human systems becomes clear. In Revelation 6, the third horseman brings with him famine and economic collapse, where even basic food items become luxuries.

EXPLANATION:

The black horse represents famine and scarcity. The scales held by the rider symbolize the careful weighing of food—an indication that resources will become scarce and will need to be rationed. A "denarius" was a day's wage in the ancient world. During this time, people would work an entire day just to afford enough food for one meal. The luxury items—oil and wine—remained untouched, showing the disparity between the wealthy and the poor.

This judgment highlights the vulnerability of humanity's economic systems. The tribulation will bring about a time when food shortages and famine are widespread, and people will struggle to survive. This rider reveals the fragility of human prosperity and security.

Yet, in the midst of this dark time, God's sovereign hand is still present. The restrictions on the oil and wine show that even in judgment, God is in control and limits the extent of the suffering.

APPLICATION:

The black horse reminds us that earthly wealth and security are fleeting. As believers, our ultimate security comes not from material wealth, but from our relationship with Christ. While the world may face scarcity and famine, we can trust in God's provision and care.

Is there an area of your life where you are relying too much on material security? Let this passage remind you that true security comes from God, not from the things of this world. Even in times of hardship, we can trust that God will provide for our needs according to His riches in glory.

FURTHER READING:

Matthew 6:31-33, Psalm 37:25, Philippians 4:19

PRAYER:

Lord, thank You for being my Provider. Help me not to place my trust in material things, but to rely on You for my daily needs. When the world faces scarcity and hardship, remind me that You are always in control and that You will never leave me nor forsake me. Amen.

CHALLENGE:

Take time today to consider areas where you may be relying too much on material security. Ask God to help you trust Him more fully in those areas, and seek ways to be generous with what you have, knowing that God is your Provider.

DAY 4: THE PALE HORSE
– DEATH AND HADES

Read Scripture: Revelation 6:7-8
Focus Scripture: Revelation 6:8 (NASB)
*"I looked, and behold, an ashen horse; and he who
sat on it had the name Death; and Hades was following with him. Authority was given to them over a fourth
of the earth, to kill with sword and with famine and
with pestilence and by the wild beasts of the earth."*

ANECDOTE:

We've all heard stories of epidemics or disasters that take many lives, reminding us of the fragility of life. The fourth horseman, Death, rides a pale horse, representing the culmination of the devastation brought by the previous riders. This horseman's arrival marks a period of unparalleled loss of life during the tribulation.

EXPLANATION:

The pale (ashen) horse represents death, and its rider is named "Death," with "Hades" following behind him. This combination symbolizes physical death and the grave. The scope of destruction is staggering. Authority is given to this rider to kill a fourth of the earth's population through war, famine, pestilence, and even attacks by wild animals.

This terrifying image reminds us of the seriousness of the coming judgments. Death will sweep across the earth, claiming countless lives, as the world faces the consequences of its rebellion against God. Yet, even in the face of this destruction, we know that God's purpose is not to destroy for the sake of destruction, but to bring about His ultimate plan of redemption and justice.

For believers, this passage underscores the urgency of the gospel. The world is heading toward a time of great suffering, and now is the time to share the hope of salvation with those who do not yet know Christ.

APPLICATION:

The pale horse reminds us that life is fragile, and that death is inevitable for everyone. But for those who are in Christ, death is not the end—it is the doorway to eternal life with God. As we reflect on this passage, we are reminded of the urgency to live for Christ and to share the gospel with others, knowing that the time is short.

Are there people in your life who do not yet know Christ? Let this passage inspire you to share the hope of salvation with them, so that they may be spared from the coming judgment and receive the gift of eternal life.

FURTHER READING:

Hebrews 9:27, 2 Corinthians 5:1, John 11:25-26

PRAYER:

Lord Jesus, thank You for the gift of eternal life. Help me to live each day with the knowledge that life is short, but death is not the end for those who trust in You. Give me the boldness to share the gospel with those who do not yet know You, and help me to live with an eternal perspective. Amen.

CHALLENGE:

Think of someone in your life who does not yet know Christ. Pray for an opportunity to share the gospel with them this week, and ask God for the courage and wisdom to speak His truth in love.

DAY 5: THE CRY OF THE MARTYRS

Read Scripture: Revelation 6:9-11
Focus Scripture: Revelation 6:10 (NASB)
"They cried out with a loud voice, saying, 'How long, O Lord, holy and true, will You refrain from judging and avenging our blood on those who dwell on the earth?'"

ANECDOTE:

Throughout history, many faithful believers have suffered persecution, even to the point of death, for their faith in Christ. In Revelation 6, we see the souls of the martyrs under the altar, crying out to God for justice. Their cries reflect the deep longing for God's righteousness to be revealed and for evil to be judged.

EXPLANATION:

The opening of the fifth seal reveals the souls of those who have been martyred for their faith in Christ. These martyrs cry out to God, asking, "How long, O Lord?" They are not seeking personal revenge, but rather they are calling for God's justice to be done. They long for the day when evil will be fully judged and righteousness will prevail.

God responds by giving them white robes, symbolizing their purity and victory, and tells them to rest for a little while longer. This response shows that God has a perfect plan and timing for everything, and that His justice will be carried out in due time.

For believers today, this passage serves as a reminder that our suffering is not in vain. God sees every injustice, every act of persecution, and He will bring justice in His time. We can trust that no matter what we face, God is in control, and He will one day make all things right.

APPLICATION:

The cry of the martyrs reminds us that, as followers of Christ, we may face persecution, but we are never forgotten by God. He sees every injustice and will bring about justice in His perfect time. This passage encourages us to remain faithful, even in the face of suffering, knowing that God is faithful and that our hope is in Him.

Are you facing challenges or opposition because of your faith? Let this passage remind you that God is with you, and that He will bring justice in His time. Stay faithful, knowing that your suffering is not in vain, and that God will reward those who stand firm in their faith.

FURTHER READING:

Matthew 5:10-12, Romans 8:18, 2 Timothy 2:12

PRAYER:

Lord, thank You for seeing every act of injustice and every instance of persecution Your people face. Help me to remain faithful, even in the face of opposition, and to trust in Your perfect timing. Thank You for the promise that You will one day make all things right. Amen.

CHALLENGE:

If you are facing any form of opposition or persecution for your faith, spend time in prayer today, asking God for strength to endure. Trust that He sees your suffering and that He will bring justice in His perfect time.

DAY 6: THE GREAT EARTHQUAKE

Read Scripture: Revelation 6:12-14
Focus Scripture: Revelation 6:12 (NASB)
"I looked when He broke the sixth seal, and there was a great earthquake; and the sun became black as sackcloth made of hair, and the whole moon became like blood."

ANECDOTE:

Earthquakes have a way of shaking us to our core, both physically and emotionally. They remind us of how fragile and temporary this world is. In Revelation 6, the opening of the sixth seal brings a great earthquake that shakes the heavens and the earth, signaling the approach of God's final judgment.

EXPLANATION:

The sixth seal unleashes cosmic disturbances—an earthquake so great that it affects not only the earth but also the heavens. The sun turns black, the moon becomes like blood, and the stars fall from the sky. These cataclysmic events are signs of the approaching judgment and the end of the world as we know it.

The imagery here is intense, showing the magnitude of God's power over creation. As the earth and the heavens shake, people will realize that they cannot escape the judgment of God. These events signal that the Day of the Lord is near, a time when God will bring justice and establish His eternal kingdom.

For believers, these signs are not meant to bring fear but rather to remind us that God's ultimate plan is being fulfilled. While the world may be shaken, our hope is secure in Christ.

APPLICATION:

The great earthquake reminds us of the power and majesty of God. While the world may face destruction and chaos we can rest in the assurance that God's kingdom is unshakable. As believers, we have the promise that no matter what happens on earth, our future with God is secure.

Are you feeling shaken by the events of the world? Let this passage remind you that God is in control, even when the world feels like it's falling apart. Take comfort in knowing that His kingdom cannot be shaken, and that He will establish His reign of peace and righteousness.

FURTHER READING:

Hebrews 12:26-28, Isaiah 13:10-13, Joel 2:30-31

PRAYER:

Lord, when the world feels like it's falling apart, help me to trust in Your unshakable kingdom. Remind me that no matter what happens, my hope is secure in You. Thank You for Your power and majesty, and for the promise that You will make all things new. Amen.

CHALLENGE:

Spend time today reflecting on God's sovereignty and power. Write down any areas of your life where you feel "shaken" and ask God to give you peace and assurance that He is in control.

DAY 7: THE WRATH OF THE LAMB

Read Scripture: Revelation 6:15-17
Focus Scripture: Revelation 6:17 (NASB)
"For the great day of their wrath has come,
and who is able to stand?"

ANECDOTE:

We often think of Jesus as the loving, gentle Shepherd, which He is. But in Revelation, we also see Him as the Lamb who pours out God's righteous wrath on a world that has rejected Him. The question asked at the end of Revelation 6 ("Who is able to stand?") reveals the severity of God's judgment, and the sobering reality of facing the wrath of the Lamb.

EXPLANATION:

As the sixth seal is broken, the world's response to the cosmic disturbances is one of fear and terror. People from every walk of life—kings, generals, the rich, and the poor—attempt to hide from the wrath of God and the Lamb. They recognize that the "great day of their wrath has come" and ask, "Who is able to stand?"

This passage reveals the seriousness of God's judgment. Those who have rejected Christ will face the full measure of God's wrath. There will be no escape, and even the most powerful people on earth will be powerless before the judgment of God.

Yet, for believers, this passage serves as a reminder of God's justice and His promise to make all things right. While the world may face God's wrath, we have the assurance that we will be spared through our faith in Christ. The Lamb who brings judgment is also the Lamb who was slain for our salvation, and it is through Him that we are able to stand.

APPLICATION:

The wrath of the Lamb is a sobering reminder of the consequences of rejecting Christ. But it is also a reminder of the incredible grace we have received through Him. We can stand before God, not because of our own righteousness, but because of the righteousness of Christ.

As you reflect on this passage, take time to thank God for the gift of salvation, and pray for those who do not yet know Christ. Let this passage motivate you to share the gospel with urgency, knowing that the time is short and that God's judgment is coming.

FURTHER READING:

Psalm 2:12, Nahum 1:6, Romans 5:9

PRAYER:

Lord Jesus, thank You for the gift of salvation and for sparing me from the wrath to come. Help me to live with an urgency to share the gospel with others, and to remain faithful as I wait for Your return. Thank You for Your justice, and for the hope that I have in You. Amen.

CHALLENGE:

Spend time in prayer for those who do not yet know Christ. Ask God to give you opportunities to share the gospel with them and pray that they will come to know Him before the day of judgment.

WEEK 6: "THE FOUR HORSEMEN OF THE APOCALYPSE"

BEYOND THE UNVEILING, GOING DEEPER

- How does the imagery of the Four Horsemen impact your understanding of the end times?

- What can you learn about God's sovereignty from the events described in this chapter?

- Reflect on how this passage challenges you to trust in God's protection and plan.

- How does the coming of the Four Horsemen increase your urgency to share the gospel?

- In what ways can you prepare your heart for the challenges of the end times?

- How does God's control over the Four Horsemen bring you comfort?

- How can this week's reading inspire you to live with a greater focus on eternity?

WEEK 7: THE SEVEN TRUMPETS OF JUDGMENT

Day 1: The First Trumpet – Hail and Fire (Revelation 8:6-7)

Day 2: The Second Trumpet – A Burning Mountain (Revelation 8:8-9)

Day 3: The Third Trumpet – The Bitter Waters (Revelation 8:10-11)

Day 4: The Fourth Trumpet – Darkness (Revelation 8:12-13)

Day 5: The Fifth Trumpet – Locusts from the Abyss (Revelation 9:1-6)

Day 6: The Sixth Trumpet – The Army of Destruction (Revelation 9:13-19)

Day 7: The Seventh Trumpet – The Kingdom of Our Lord (Revelation 11:15-19)

DAY 1: THE FIRST TRUMPET – HAIL AND FIRE

Read Scripture: Revelation 8:6-7
Focus Scripture: Revelation 8:7 (NASB)
*"The first sounded, and there came hail and fire, mixed
with blood, and they were thrown to the earth; and a third
of the earth was burned up, and a third of the trees were
burned up, and all the green grass was burned up."*

ANECDOTE:

Imagine a summer storm, powerful and fierce. Hailstones pelt the ground, and flashes of lightning ignite fires that spread rapidly. Now imagine this scene on a global scale, with devastating destruction. The first trumpet in Revelation brings a judgment of hail and fire, signaling the beginning of catastrophic devastation on the earth.

EXPLANATION:

As the first angel sounds the trumpet, a judgment of hail and fire mixed with blood is cast upon the earth. The result is devastating: a third of the earth, trees, and all green grass are burned up. This imagery reminds us of the plagues that fell on Egypt (Exodus 9:22-25), where God used hail as a form of judgment. However, this judgment is far more intense and widespread.

This first trumpet sets the stage for the escalating judgments that will follow. The earth, which once sustained life, is now suffering under the weight of God's wrath as a result of humanity's sin. The burning of the earth is a reminder of the fragility of the natural world and how creation itself suffers the consequences of human rebellion.

Yet even in the midst of this judgment, God's mercy is evident. Only a third of the earth is affected, indicating that God is still offering humanity an opportunity to repent before the final judgment.

APPLICATION:

The first trumpet reminds us that the created world is not immune to the effects of sin and judgment. While this passage speaks of future events, it also serves as a reminder that our world is fragile and that everything we see around us is temporary. We are called to live with an eternal perspective, focusing on the things that matter most—our relationship with God and the hope of eternal life.

Are there areas in your life where you are too focused on temporary things? Let this passage remind you to invest in what is eternal, knowing that the things of this world will one day pass away.

FURTHER READING:

2 Peter 3:10-13, Matthew 6:19-21, Romans 8:20-22

PRAYER:

Lord, thank You for reminding me that this world is temporary and that my hope is in You. Help me to live with an eternal perspective, investing in the things that matter most. Thank You for Your mercy and patience, even in the midst of judgment. Amen.

CHALLENGE:

Take time today to reflect on your priorities. Are you investing in things that will last for eternity? Make a commitment to focus more on your relationship with God and less on the temporary things of this world.

DAY 2: THE SECOND TRUMPET – A BURNING MOUNTAIN

Read Scripture: Revelation 8:8-9
Focus Scripture: Revelation 8:8 (NASB)
*"The second angel sounded, and something like a
great mountain burning with fire was thrown into
the sea; and a third of the sea became blood."*

ANECDOTE:

Volcanic eruptions are some of the most powerful and terrifying forces in nature. When a mountain erupts, the surrounding area is devastated by fire and ash, and the sea can turn deadly. In Revelation, the second trumpet brings an event even more catastrophic—a burning mountain that is thrown into the sea, causing widespread destruction.

EXPLANATION:

When the second trumpet sounds, John sees something "like a great mountain" burning with fire being cast into the sea. The result is devastating: a third of the sea becomes blood, a third of the sea creatures die, and a third of the ships are destroyed. This imagery recalls the plague of blood in Egypt (Exodus 7:20-21), but on a much larger scale.

The burning mountain represents a cataclysmic event that impacts the world's oceans, which are essential for sustaining life on earth. The transformation of the sea into blood and the death of marine life signify the severity of God's judgment on creation. The destruction of ships also points to the economic consequences, as maritime trade and transportation are crippled.

Yet, as with the first trumpet, we see God's mercy in that only a third of the sea is affected. This partial judgment is a warning to humanity, giving them an opportunity to repent before the final judgment comes.

APPLICATION:

The second trumpet reminds us of the interconnectedness of creation and how quickly things can unravel when God's judgment is unleashed. The sea, which is often a symbol of stability and abundance, is turned into a place of death and destruction. This passage challenges us to consider how much we rely on the things of this world for security, rather than on God.

Are there areas in your life where you are placing your trust in earthly things instead of in God? Let this passage remind you to place your hope and security in Christ alone, knowing that everything in this world is temporary.

FURTHER READING:

Psalm 46:2-3, Isaiah 24:4-6, Colossians 3:1-3

PRAYER:

Lord, help me to place my trust in You rather than in the things of this world. Thank You for reminding me that this world is not my home, and that my hope is in You. Help me to live with confidence in Your eternal promises, even in the midst of uncertainty. Amen.

CHALLENGE:

Examine your life for areas where you may be relying too much on earthly things for security. Ask God to help you place your trust fully in Him and to live with a heart focused on eternity.

DAY 3: THE THIRD TRUMPET – THE BITTER WATERS

Read Scripture: Revelation 8:10-11
Focus Scripture: Revelation 8:11 (NASB)
*"The name of the star is called Wormwood; and a third
of the waters became wormwood, and many men died
from the waters, because they were made bitter."*

ANECDOTE:

Think of a time when you were desperately thirsty, only to find that the water available to you was contaminated and undrinkable. This is the tragic scenario described in the third trumpet judgment, where a star named Wormwood falls to the earth, turning the waters bitter and undrinkable, leading to widespread death.

EXPLANATION:

The third trumpet reveals a great star, called Wormwood, falling from heaven. This star impacts the rivers and springs of water, turning a third of the fresh water bitter and poisonous. Many people die as a result of drinking the contaminated water.

Wormwood is a bitter plant, often associated with sorrow and judgment in Scripture (Jeremiah 9:15, Lamentations 3:19). The name of the star emphasizes the bitterness of the judgment that falls upon the earth. Water, which is essential for life, is now a source of death. This judgment affects the basic necessities of life, reminding humanity of their dependence on God for even the most fundamental resources.

Once again, God's mercy is evident in the fact that only a third of the waters are affected. This is a partial judgment, meant to serve as a warning to the world of the greater judgment to come if they do not repent.

APPLICATION:

The third trumpet reminds us of how fragile life is and how dependent we are on God's provision. Water is something we often take for granted, yet in this passage, we see how quickly it can become a source of death rather than life. This judgment serves as a reminder to turn to God, the true source of life and sustenance.

Are you relying on God as your source of life or are you seeking satisfaction in other things? Let this passage remind you that true life comes only from God, and that apart from Him, everything is bitter and unsatisfying.

FURTHER READING:

John 4:13-14, Jeremiah 2:13, Revelation 22:1-2

PRAYER:

Lord, thank You for being the source of living water. Help me to turn to You for all my needs, and to rely on Your provision and grace. Remind me that nothing in this world can truly satisfy, and that true life is found only in You. Amen.

CHALLENGE:

Take time today to reflect on areas where you may be seeking satisfaction apart from God. Ask Him to help you turn to Him as the source of true life and commit to spending more time in His presence this week.

DAY 4: THE FOURTH TRUMPET – DARKNESS

Read Scripture: Revelation 8:12-13
Focus Scripture: Revelation 8:12 (NASB)
*"The fourth angel sounded, and a third of the sun and a
third of the moon and a third of the stars were struck, so that
a third of them would be darkened and the day would not
shine for a third of it, and the night in the same way."*

ANECDOTE:

Have you ever experienced a sudden power outage at night, where
the darkness was so deep it felt disorienting? In the fourth trumpet, the
lights of the heavens—the sun, moon, and stars—are darkened, plunging
the world into a time of deep spiritual and physical darkness.

EXPLANATION:

The fourth trumpet brings a judgment that strikes the heavens. A
third of the sun, moon, and stars are darkened, causing a significant reduction in light on the earth. This judgment echoes the ninth plague in
Egypt (Exodus 10:21-23), where darkness fell upon the land for three
days. Darkness in the Bible often represents judgment and separation
from God's presence.

This reduction in light affects both the day and the night, disrupt-
ing the natural order and causing widespread fear and confusion. The
darkness also symbolizes the increasing spiritual blindness that will grip
the earth during the tribulation. As the judgments intensify, humanity's
rejection of God becomes more evident, and the darkness of their hearts
is reflected in the physical darkness around them.

APPLICATION:

The fourth trumpet reminds us of the seriousness of spiritual darkness. Just as physical darkness can be disorienting and frightening, spiritual darkness leads to confusion, fear, and separation from God. As believers, we are called to walk in the light of Christ and to share that light with others.

Are you walking in the light of Christ, or are there areas of your life where spiritual darkness has crept in? Let this passage remind you of the importance of staying close to Jesus, the Light of the World, and shining His light in a darkened world.

FURTHER READING:

John 8:12, Isaiah 60:1-2, Ephesians 5:8-11

PRAYER:

Lord Jesus, thank You for being the Light of the World. Help me to walk in Your light and to avoid the darkness of sin and confusion. Give me the courage to shine Your light in the world, and to point others to You, especially in times of darkness. Amen.

CHALLENGE:

Identify an area in your life where you need to walk more fully in the light of Christ. Ask God to help you overcome any darkness and look for opportunities to be a light to those around you this week.

DAY 5: THE FIFTH TRUMPET – LOCUSTS FROM THE ABYSS

Read Scripture: Revelation 9:1-6
Focus Scripture: Revelation 9:3 (NASB)
"Then out of the smoke came locusts upon the earth, and power was given them, as the scorpions of the earth have power."

ANECDOTE:

Have you ever experienced a swarm of insects, like locusts, where it seemed like they took over everything? It can be terrifying and overwhelming. In Revelation 9, we see a judgment where locust-like creatures emerge from the abyss, but these are no ordinary locusts. They bring not just destruction to crops but torment to people, a vivid picture of the terror of God's judgment.

EXPLANATION:

The fifth trumpet introduces a terrifying vision: a star falls from heaven to earth, and the "key to the bottomless pit" is given to this fallen star, likely a reference to a powerful demonic figure or Satan himself. When the abyss is opened, smoke rises, and from this smoke comes a swarm of locust-like creatures. These creatures, however, are not ordinary locusts. They are given the power to torment people, like scorpions, but they are forbidden from killing. Their torment lasts for five months, and their victims long for death, but death eludes them.

These locusts symbolize a demonic plague that brings extreme physical and emotional suffering. Their emergence from the abyss shows that this is a supernatural judgment, with the torment coming from the forces of darkness. The fact that people seek death but cannot find it reflects the despair and hopelessness that comes with rejecting God.

Yet even in this judgment, God's mercy is evident. The locusts are limited in their power and time, showing that God is still in control, even during this time of great suffering.

APPLICATION:

The fifth trumpet reminds us of the reality of spiritual warfare and the consequences of turning away from God. The torment experienced by those on the earth is a vivid picture of the emptiness and despair that come from living apart from God. But as believers, we are not subject to this judgment because we are sealed and protected by Christ.

Is there an area of your life where you are experiencing spiritual attack or torment? Let this passage remind you that God is your protector, and that through Christ, you have victory over the forces of darkness. If you are facing spiritual warfare, turn to Jesus for strength and protection, knowing that He has overcome the enemy.

FURTHER READING:

Ephesians 6:10-12, 1 Peter 5:8-9, 1 John 4:4

PRAYER:

Lord Jesus, thank You for being my protector and for giving me victory over the forces of darkness. Help me to stand firm in my faith and to trust in Your strength when I face spiritual battles. Remind me that in You, I have nothing to fear. Amen.

CHALLENGE:

If you are facing any form of spiritual attack, spend time in prayer today, asking God for protection and strength. Commit to wearing the full armor of God (Ephesians 6) and standing firm in the victory that Jesus has already won for you.

DAY 6: THE SIXTH TRUMPET – THE ARMY OF DESTRUCTION

Read Scripture: Revelation 9:13-19
Focus Scripture: Revelation 9:15 (NASB)
"And the four angels, who had been prepared for the hour and day and month and year, were released, so that they would kill a third of mankind."

ANECDOTE:

Imagine a scene where an army so vast and destructive sweeps across a land, leaving death and destruction in its wake. The sixth trumpet brings such a vision, where an army of destruction is unleashed upon the world, resulting in the death of a third of humanity.

EXPLANATION:

The sixth trumpet introduces the release of four angels who have been bound at the great river Euphrates. These angels are described as being prepared for a specific moment in history—"the hour and day and month and year"—indicating God's precise control over the timing of this judgment. When these angels are released, they lead an army of 200 million horsemen who bring destruction and death to a third of the world's population.

This vision is both terrifying and sobering. The vast army of horsemen, with their grotesque and deadly appearance, symbolizes the intensity of the judgment that is unleashed. Fire, smoke, and brimstone are described as the means by which the horsemen kill, reminiscent of the destruction of Sodom and Gomorrah (Genesis 19:24). The scale of death and destruction is unlike anything the world has ever seen.

The fact that the angels were prepared for this specific time shows us that nothing happens outside of God's sovereign plan. Even in the midst of such devastation, God is in control, and His purposes are being fulfilled.

APPLICATION:

The sixth trumpet is a powerful reminder of God's sovereignty, even in the midst of judgment. The vast destruction caused by the army of horsemen highlights the seriousness of sin and the consequences of rejecting God. Yet, for believers, this passage also reminds us that we are under God's protection and that His plan is always good, even when the world seems out of control.

Are you feeling overwhelmed by the events of the world or the challenges in your life? Let this passage remind you that God is in control, even in the darkest of times. His purposes will be fulfilled, and He will protect and preserve those who trust in Him.

FURTHER READING:

Psalm 91:1-4, Isaiah 41:10, Romans 8:28

PRAYER:

Lord, thank You for being in control, even when the world seems chaotic and out of control. Help me to trust in Your sovereignty and to find peace in knowing that You are working all things for good. Thank You for being my protector and my refuge in times of trouble. Amen.

CHALLENGE:

Take time today to reflect on God's sovereignty in your life. Are there areas where you need to trust Him more fully? Surrender those areas to Him, knowing that He is in control and that His plan is always good.

DAY 7: THE SEVENTH TRUMPET – THE KINGDOM OF OUR LORD

Read Scripture: Revelation 11:15-19
Focus Scripture: Revelation 11:15 (NASB)
"Then the seventh angel sounded; and there were loud voices in heaven, saying, 'The kingdom of the world has become the kingdom of our Lord and of His Christ; and He will reign forever and ever.'"

ANECDOTE:

Have you ever waited for a moment of victory, whether in a competition, a battle, or even the resolution of a long struggle? The seventh trumpet marks the ultimate moment of victory in Revelation, as the kingdom of the world becomes the kingdom of Christ, and His eternal reign is established.

EXPLANATION:

The seventh trumpet brings a glorious announcement: the kingdom of the world has become the kingdom of our Lord and His Christ. This marks the moment when Jesus' victory is fully realized, and His reign is established over all creation. The loud voices in heaven proclaim the eternal reign of Christ, and the twenty-four elders fall on their faces in worship, giving thanks to God for His great power and justice.

The seventh trumpet also brings the announcement that God's judgment has come. The time has arrived for the dead to be judged, for rewards to be given to God's faithful servants, and for the destruction of those who have opposed Him. This marks the final phase of God's redemptive plan, where all things are made right, and the kingdom of Christ is established forever.

For believers, the sound of the seventh trumpet is a moment of great joy and hope. It is the culmination of all that we have waited for: the establishment of God's eternal kingdom, where there will be no more sin, suffering, or death. This is the hope that sustains us as we endure the trials and challenges of this life.

APPLICATION:

The seventh trumpet reminds us of the ultimate victory of Christ. No matter what we face in this world, we can have confidence that Jesus will reign forever and that His kingdom will be established in full. This truth gives us hope and endurance, knowing that our future is secure in Christ.

Are you living in light of Christ's eternal reign? Let this passage remind you that no matter how difficult life may be, Jesus is victorious, and His kingdom will never be shaken. Live each day with the hope of eternity, knowing that you are part of His eternal kingdom.

FURTHER READING:

Daniel 7:13-14, 1 Corinthians 15:24-25, Hebrews 12:28

PRAYER:

Lord Jesus, thank You for the promise of Your eternal reign. Help me to live each day with the hope and confidence that You are victorious, and that Your kingdom will never be shaken. Thank You for the joy of knowing that I am part of Your eternal kingdom. Amen.

CHALLENGE:

Spend time today reflecting on the hope of Christ's eternal kingdom. How does this truth impact the way you live your life? Ask God to help you live with greater confidence in His victory and to share this hope with others.

WEEK 7: "THE SEVEN TRUMPETS OF JUDGMENT"

BEYOND THE UNVEILING, GOING DEEPER

- How does the imagery of the trumpets help you understand the seriousness of God's judgment?

- What response does this chapter evoke in you regarding God's power and justice?

- How does the vision of judgment motivate you to pray for others?

- What lessons about intercession can you draw from the events of the trumpets?

- Reflect on a time when God's warnings changed your course. How did you respond?

- How can this week's passages encourage you to live with greater urgency for God's mission?

- In what ways can you make a renewed commitment to share the hope of salvation with others?

WEEK 8: THE SEVEN BOWLS OF GOD'S WRATH

DAY 1: THE FIRST BOWL – PAINFUL SORES (REVELATION 16:1-2)

DAY 2: THE SECOND BOWL – THE SEA TURNS TO BLOOD (REVELATION 16:3)

DAY 3: THE THIRD BOWL – THE RIVERS AND SPRINGS BECOME BLOOD (REVELATION 16:4-7)

DAY 4: THE FOURTH BOWL – SCORCHING HEAT (REVELATION 16:8-9)

DAY 5: THE FIFTH BOWL – DARKNESS OVER THE KINGDOM (REVELATION 16:10-11)

DAY 6: THE SIXTH BOWL – THE RIVER EUPHRATES DRIED UP (REVELATION 16:12-16)

DAY 7: THE SEVENTH BOWL – "IT IS DONE" (REVELATION 16:17-21)

DAY 1: THE FIRST BOWL – PAINFUL SORES

Read Scripture: Revelation 16:1-2
Focus Scripture: Revelation 16:2 (NASB)
"So the first angel went and poured out his bowl on the earth;
and it became a loathsome and malignant sore on the people
who had the mark of the beast and who worshiped his image."

ANECDOTE:

Imagine experiencing a painful skin condition that leaves you in constant agony, with no relief in sight. The first bowl of God's wrath brings painful sores on those who have rejected Christ and chosen to follow the beast. These sores are a visible and painful reminder of the consequences of rejecting God's grace.

EXPLANATION:

The first bowl of God's wrath is poured out upon the earth, and it results in "loathsome and malignant" sores afflicting those who bear the mark of the beast and worship his image. This judgment is targeted specifically at those who have chosen to reject God and align themselves with the Antichrist. The painful sores are reminiscent of the boils that plagued Egypt (Exodus 9:8-12), but here, they serve as a sign of the deeper spiritual affliction of those who have turned away from God.

The physical pain caused by the sores reflects the spiritual reality of those who have chosen to follow the beast. They are experiencing the consequences of their rebellion against God, and these sores are just the beginning of the suffering they will endure during the final judgments.

APPLICATION:

The first bowl reminds us that there are real consequences to rejecting God. While this passage speaks of future events, it also serves as a warning to us today. God's desire is that all would come to repentance, but those who continue to reject His grace will face judgment.

Is there an area of your life where you are resisting God's will? Let this passage remind you of the importance of submitting to Him and walking in obedience to His Word. God's judgments are just, but His grace is available to all who turn to Him.

FURTHER READING:

Exodus 9:8-12, Isaiah 1:4-6, 2 Thessalonians 2:9-12

PRAYER:

Lord, thank You for Your grace and patience. Help me to walk in obedience to You and to turn away from anything that draws me away from Your will. Thank You for being a God of both justice and mercy. Amen.

CHALLENGE:

Reflect on areas in your life where you may be resisting God's will. Surrender those areas to Him today, asking for His grace to help you walk in obedience.

DAY 2: THE SECOND BOWL – THE SEA TURNS TO BLOOD

Read Scripture: Revelation 16:3
Focus Scripture: Revelation 16:3 (NASB)
"The second angel poured out his bowl into the sea, and it became blood like that of a dead man; and every living thing in the sea died."

ANECDOTE:

Consider the beauty and life-giving power of the ocean, filled with vibrant creatures and ecosystems. Now imagine that same sea turning into a vast expanse of blood, lifeless and toxic. This is the devastating result of the second bowl judgment, where the sea becomes a place of death rather than life.

EXPLANATION:

The second bowl of God's wrath is poured into the sea, and the entire sea turns into blood, "like that of a dead man." The result is the death of every living thing in the sea. This judgment is reminiscent of the first plague in Egypt, where the Nile River was turned to blood (Exodus 7:20-21). However, this judgment is global in scope, affecting the entire sea and leading to the death of all marine life.

The sea, once a source of life and sustenance, now becomes a symbol of death and decay. This judgment reflects the severity of God's wrath against those who have rejected Him and chosen to follow the beast. The turning of the sea into blood is a powerful reminder that God is not only the Creator but also the Judge of all creation.

APPLICATION:

The second bowl reminds us that even creation itself is affected by human sin and rebellion. The sea, which was once teeming with life, is now a place of death. This passage challenges us to reflect on the impact of sin, not only on our lives but on the world around us.

As believers, we are called to care for God's creation and to live in a way that honors Him. Are there areas of your life where you are contributing to the brokenness of creation or ignoring the consequences of sin? Let this passage remind you to live in a way that reflects God's holiness and righteousness.

FURTHER READING:

Romans 8:19-22, Isaiah 24:4-6, Psalm 104:24-30

PRAYER:

Lord, thank You for being both the Creator and the Judge of all creation. Help me to live in a way that honors You and to recognize the impact of sin on the world around me. Thank You for Your grace and for the hope that one day You will make all things new. Amen.

CHALLENGE:

Take time today to reflect on how you are caring for God's creation. Are there ways you can live more responsibly, recognizing that all of creation belongs to Him? Commit to making a small change this week that reflects your desire to honor God in how you live.

DAY 3: THE THIRD BOWL – THE RIVERS AND SPRINGS BECOME BLOOD

Read Scripture: Revelation 16:4-7
Focus Scripture: Revelation 16:6 (NASB)
"For they poured out the blood of saints and prophets, and You have given them blood to drink. They deserve it."

ANECDOTE:

Imagine turning on your faucet to find that instead of water, blood flows from the tap. The shock and horror would be overwhelming. In the third bowl judgment, the rivers and springs of water turn to blood, reflecting God's judgment on a world that has shed the blood of His people.

EXPLANATION:

The third bowl of God's wrath is poured out on the rivers and springs of water, and they become blood. This judgment affects the fresh water sources, making it impossible for people to drink. The angel declares that this judgment is just because the world has shed the blood of God's people, His saints and prophets. Now, they are given blood to drink as a reflection of the blood they have shed.

This passage highlights the principle of divine justice: what the world has done to God's people is now being done to them. The persecution and martyrdom of believers are met with God's righteous judgment, and the angel's declaration, "They deserve it," shows that God's judgments are always fair and just.

For believers, this passage is a reminder that God sees every injustice and act of persecution. He will one day make all things right, and His judgment will be perfectly righteous.

APPLICATION:

The third bowl reminds us that God's justice is sure and that He will avenge the blood of His people. While we may face persecution or suffering in this life, we can trust that God sees and will bring justice in His time. This passage also challenges us to live righteously, knowing that God's judgment is fair and that He will reward those who remain faithful.

Are you facing challenges or opposition because of your faith? Let this passage encourage you to remain steadfast, knowing that God sees your faithfulness and will bring justice in His perfect time.

FURTHER READING:

Deuteronomy 32:43, Romans 12:19, 2 Thessalonians 1:6-7

PRAYER:

Lord, thank You for being a God of justice and righteousness. Help me to remain faithful, even in the face of opposition or persecution. Thank You for the promise that You see every injustice, and that You will bring justice in Your perfect time. Amen.

CHALLENGE:

If you are facing opposition or persecution for your faith, take time today to pray for strength and endurance. Trust that God sees your faithfulness and that He will reward you for standing firm in Him.

DAY 4: THE FOURTH BOWL – SCORCHING HEAT

Read Scripture: Revelation 16:8-9
Focus Scripture: Revelation 16:9 (NASB)
*"Men were scorched with fierce heat; and they blasphemed
the name of God who has the power over these plagues,
and they did not repent so as to give Him glory."*

ANECDOTE:

We've all experienced the discomfort of an extremely hot day, where the sun feels unbearable and all you want is to find shade. Now imagine the heat being so intense that it feels inescapable and deadly. The fourth bowl of God's wrath brings a scorching heat upon the earth that is so severe it causes people to suffer deeply.

EXPLANATION:

The fourth bowl judgment causes the sun to scorch people with intense heat. This is a direct judgment on creation, where the very source of light and warmth becomes a source of pain and suffering. What's striking is the response of those afflicted by this judgment: instead of repenting, they blaspheme the name of God.

This passage highlights the hardness of the human heart. Even in the face of such overwhelming evidence of God's power, people refuse to repent. Their suffering, rather than leading to repentance, leads to further rebellion against God.

The scorching heat also reflects the reality of God's judgment: it is both physical and spiritual. Those who reject God's grace experience the consequences of that rejection, not only in this life but in the judgment to come.

APPLICATION:

The fourth bowl challenges us to consider the state of our hearts. Are we open to God's correction and leading, or are we resistant to His will? This passage serves as a warning to not harden our hearts when God calls us to repent. His desire is for us to turn to Him and find healing, but if we continue to reject Him, we will experience the consequences of that choice.

Is there an area in your life where you are resisting God's correction? Let this passage remind you that God's judgment is real, but so is His grace. Turn to Him in repentance, and allow His light to bring healing and restoration to your life.

FURTHER READING:

Isaiah 24:6, 2 Peter 3:10, Hebrews 3:7-8

PRAYER:

Lord, help me to have a heart that is soft and open to Your correction. Forgive me for the times I have resisted Your will and help me to walk in repentance and obedience. Thank You for being a God of mercy and grace even in the midst of judgment. Amen.

CHALLENGE:

Spend time in reflection today, asking God to reveal any areas of your life where you may be resisting His will. Commit to surrendering those areas to Him and walking in obedience.

DAY 5: THE FIFTH BOWL – DARKNESS OVER THE KINGDOM

Read Scripture: Revelation 16:10-11
Focus Scripture: Revelation 16:10 (NASB)
*"Then the fifth angel poured out his bowl on the throne
of the beast, and his kingdom became darkened; and
they gnawed their tongues because of pain."*

ANECDOTE:

Imagine being plunged into complete darkness, where the absence of light is so overwhelming that it creates physical and emotional distress. The fifth bowl judgment brings such darkness upon the kingdom of the beast, causing intense suffering and despair among those who follow him.

EXPLANATION:

The fifth bowl of God's wrath is poured out on the throne of the beast, and his kingdom is plunged into darkness. This judgment is a direct attack on the kingdom of the Antichrist, showing the powerlessness of his reign in the face of God's authority. The darkness is so intense that people "gnaw their tongues because of pain," a vivid description of their torment.

What's particularly tragic is that, once again, instead of repenting, the people continue to blaspheme God. The darkness symbolizes both physical and spiritual blindness—those who follow the beast are not only in physical darkness but also in spiritual darkness, refusing to turn to the light of God.

This judgment reminds us that any kingdom or power that stands in opposition to God will ultimately be brought low. The reign of the Antichrist, though seemingly powerful, is no match for the authority of God, and it will end in utter darkness and defeat.

APPLICATION:

The fifth bowl challenges us to examine where we are placing our trust. Are we aligning ourselves with the kingdom of God, or are we putting our hope in the things of this world? The kingdom of the beast is destined for darkness and destruction, but the kingdom of God is a kingdom of light and life.

Are there areas in your life where you are trusting in things that are not of God? Let this passage remind you that only God's kingdom will stand, and only those who walk in His light will experience true life and peace.

FURTHER READING:

John 12:35-36, 1 John 1:5-7, Matthew 25:30

PRAYER:

Lord, thank You for being the Light of the World. Help me to walk in Your light and to turn away from anything that leads me into darkness. Thank You for the promise that Your kingdom is a kingdom of light and that I can trust in You completely. Amen.

CHALLENGE:

Take time today to reflect on areas where you may be walking in spiritual darkness. Ask God to help you turn fully to His light and commit to living in alignment with His kingdom.

DAY 6: THE SIXTH BOWL – THE RIVER EUPHRATES DRIED UP

Read Scripture: Revelation 16:12-16
Focus Scripture: Revelation 16:12 (NASB)
"The sixth angel poured out his bowl on the great river, the Euphrates; and its water was dried up, so that the way would be prepared for the kings from the east."

ANECDOTE:

Rivers often symbolize life and abundance, providing water for people and agriculture. But what happens when a great river dries up? The sixth bowl of God's wrath sees the drying up of the Euphrates River, not as a natural disaster, but as a divine preparation for the final conflict between good and evil.

EXPLANATION:

The sixth bowl is poured out on the Euphrates River, causing its waters to dry up. This prepares the way for the kings from the east to gather for the final battle, often referred to as Armageddon. The drying of the river, a natural barrier, allows armies to cross and positions the forces of evil for their ultimate defeat at the hands of God.

This judgment is not only physical but also spiritual, as demonic spirits are released to deceive the kings of the earth, leading them to gather for war against God. This is a critical moment in the unfolding of God's plan, as the forces of evil are being set up for their final defeat.

The drying up of the Euphrates also reflects the sovereignty of God. Even in the midst of judgment, He is orchestrating events to bring about His ultimate victory. What may seem like a moment of chaos is, in reality, God preparing the way for His final triumph over evil.

APPLICATION:

The sixth bowl reminds us that God is in control, even in times of great conflict and uncertainty. While the world may be heading toward a final battle, we can trust that God's victory is assured. This passage challenges us to live with confidence in God's sovereignty, knowing that He is always working to bring about His perfect plan.

Are you facing situations that feel like a battle in your own life? Let this passage remind you that God is in control, even when things seem uncertain. Trust in His timing and His plan, knowing that His victory is already won.

FURTHER READING:

Psalm 46:8-11, Isaiah 40:23-24, Revelation 19:11-16

PRAYER:

Lord, thank You for being in control of every situation, even the battles I face. Help me to trust in Your timing and Your plan, knowing that Your victory is certain. Give me peace in the midst of uncertainty and help me to walk in faith as I wait for Your final triumph. Amen.

CHALLENGE:

Identify a situation in your life that feels like a battle. Surrender it to God today, trusting that He is in control and that His victory is assured.

DAY 7: THE SEVENTH BOWL – "IT IS DONE"

Read Scripture: Revelation 16:17-21
Focus Scripture: Revelation 16:17 (NASB)
*"Then the seventh angel poured out his bowl upon
the air, and a loud voice came out of the temple from the throne, saying, 'It is done.'"*

ANECDOTE:

Think of a time when you completed a long and challenging project. The sense of accomplishment and finality can bring great relief. In Revelation 16:17, the seventh bowl is poured out, and a loud voice from the throne declares, "It is done." This marks the completion of God's judgment and the beginning of His final victory.

EXPLANATION:

The seventh bowl is poured out into the air, and with it comes a declaration from God's throne: "It is done." This echoes Jesus' words on the cross, "It is finished" (John 19:30), marking the completion of His work of salvation. Now, with this final judgment, God's plan of justice is complete, and the stage is set for the return of Christ.

The seventh bowl brings great earthquakes, hailstones, and the destruction of cities. The wrath of God is fully poured out, and the kingdom of this world is shaken to its core. The power and authority of God are on full display as He brings an end to the reign of sin and rebellion.

For believers, the declaration "It is done" is a reminder that God's victory is certain. The suffering and trials of this world will not last forever. God will bring His justice, and His kingdom will be fully established.

APPLICATION:

The seventh bowl reminds us that God's justice will be complete. While we may face trials and difficulties in this life, we can have confidence that God's plan is unfolding, and His victory is assured. This passage challenges us to live in light of that victory, trusting that the day will come when all things will be made new.

Are you feeling weary from the challenges of this world? Let this passage encourage you to hold on to the hope of God's final victory. "It is done" reminds us that God's plan is already finished, and we are on the winning side.

FURTHER READING:

John 19:30, Revelation 21:5-7, Romans 8:18

PRAYER:

Lord, thank You for the promise that "it is done." Help me to live each day with confidence in Your victory, knowing that Your plan is perfect and complete. Give me the strength to endure the trials of this life, and help me to live in the hope of Your eternal kingdom. Amen.

CHALLENGE:

Reflect on the hope of God's final victory today. Write down any challenges or trials you are facing, and surrender them to God, trusting in His ultimate plan and victory.

WEEK 8: "THE SEVEN BOWLS OF GOD'S WRATH"

BEYOND THE UNVEILING, GOING DEEPER

- How does the imagery of the bowls of wrath reveal the weight of unrepentant sin?

- What does this passage teach you about the importance of repentance?

- How do these judgments challenge you to revere God's holiness?

- How does knowing that God's wrath will be fully executed affect your understanding of justice?

- How can this week's passages deepen your gratitude for salvation through Christ?

- How does the promise of God's ultimate judgment give you peace amid today's injustices?

- How can you demonstrate compassion and urgency to those who have yet to receive Christ?

WEEK 9: BABYLON THE GREAT AND THE FALL OF EVIL

DAY 1: THE WOMAN ON THE SCARLET BEAST (REVELATION 17:1-6)

DAY 2: THE MYSTERY OF BABYLON THE GREAT (REVELATION 17:7-14)

DAY 3: THE FALL OF BABYLON (REVELATION 17:15-18)

DAY 4: THE KINGS LAMENT BABYLON'S DESTRUCTION (REVELATION 18:9-10)

DAY 5: REJOICING IN HEAVEN OVER BABYLON'S FALL (REVELATION 18:20-24)

DAY 6: THE VOICE FROM HEAVEN (REVELATION 18:1-8)

DAY 7: THE JUDGMENT OF BABYLON COMPLETE (REVELATION 19:1-5)

DAY 1: THE WOMAN ON THE SCARLET BEAST

Read Scripture: Revelation 17:1-6
Focus Scripture: Revelation 17:3 (NASB)
*"And he carried me away in the Spirit into a wilderness;
and I saw a woman sitting on a scarlet beast, full of blasphemous names, having seven heads and ten horns."*

ANECDOTE:

Imagine coming across a powerful and striking figure, someone who exudes influence and wealth, yet there's something unsettling about them—an aura of corruption and danger. In Revelation 17, we see a vision of a woman clothed in luxury, riding a scarlet beast. But this woman represents something far more sinister: the corrupt world system known as Babylon the Great.

EXPLANATION:

The vision of the woman on the scarlet beast introduces us to Babylon the Great, a symbolic representation of the world system that opposes God. The woman is described as being adorned in purple and scarlet, with gold, precious stones, and pearls—symbols of wealth, power, and influence. Yet, despite her outward appearance, she is "drunk with the blood of the saints," revealing the true nature of her wickedness.

The beast she rides is covered in blasphemous names and has seven heads and ten horns, representing the worldly kingdoms and powers that align themselves against God. This vision reveals the intimate connection between the world's corrupt systems and the powers of darkness. Babylon the Great represents not only political and economic corruption but also spiritual deception, leading many astray from the truth of God.

As we encounter this vision, we are reminded that what appears alluring and powerful in this world may be deeply corrupt. The wealth and influence of Babylon are temporary, and her judgment is coming.

APPLICATION:

The vision of the woman on the scarlet beast challenges us to examine where we place our trust and allegiance. Are we drawn to the wealth and influence of the world, or are we standing firm in our commitment to Christ? Babylon the Great represents all that is opposed to God, and those who follow her path will face judgment.

Is there an area of your life where you may be compromising with the values of this world? Let this passage remind you to stand firm in your faith, resisting the temptations of wealth, power, and influence that are contrary to God's kingdom.

FURTHER READING:

1 John 2:15-17, James 4:4, 1 Timothy 6:9-10

PRAYER:

Lord, help me to see through the deception of this world and to resist the temptations of wealth and power that lead me away from You. Strengthen my commitment to stand firm in my faith and to live according to Your values, not the world's. Amen.

CHALLENGE:

Reflect on areas in your life where you may be compromising with the world's values. Ask God to help you stand firm in His truth and resist the influence of Babylon in your life.

DAY 2: THE MYSTERY OF BABYLON THE GREAT

Read Scripture: Revelation 17:7-14
Focus Scripture: Revelation 17:14 (NASB)
"These will wage war against the Lamb, and the Lamb will overcome them, because He is Lord of lords and King of kings, and those who are with Him are the called and chosen and faithful."

ANECDOTE:

In many stories of battle or conflict there is often a moment when it seems like the enemy has the upper hand. But then the tide turns, and the hero emerges victorious. Revelation 17 paints a similar picture as the powers of darkness align against Christ, only to be utterly defeated by the Lamb, who is King of kings and Lord of lords.

EXPLANATION:

In this passage, the angel explains to John the mystery of the woman and the beast. The seven heads and ten horns of the beast represent various kingdoms and rulers that will align themselves against God's people. These rulers will wage war against the Lamb, symbolizing the ultimate rebellion of the world system against Christ.

However, the outcome of this conflict is already certain. The Lamb will overcome them, because He is the Lord of lords and King of kings. The power of the beast and the rulers of this world is no match for the authority of Christ. His victory is sure, and those who are with Him—His faithful followers—will share in His triumph.

This passage serves as both a warning and an encouragement. It reminds us that there will be times when the forces of darkness seem powerful, but we must remember that Christ has already won the victory. No matter how fierce the opposition, Jesus will overcome, and those who remain faithful to Him will share in His victory.

APPLICATION:

The mystery of Babylon the Great challenges us to remain faithful, even when the world seems to be aligned against us. The powers of darkness may appear strong, but they cannot stand against the Lamb. As believers, we are called to persevere, knowing that our victory is already secured in Christ.

Are you facing opposition or feeling discouraged by the state of the world? Let this passage remind you that Christ is victorious and that you are part of His kingdom. Stand firm in your faith, knowing that nothing can separate you from His love and victory.

FURTHER READING:

Romans 8:37-39, 1 Timothy 6:15, Philippians 2:9-11

PRAYER:

Lord Jesus, thank You for being the victorious Lamb, the King of kings and Lord of lords. Help me to stand firm in my faith, even when the world is against me. Strengthen me to persevere, knowing that You have already won the victory. Amen.

CHALLENGE:

If you are facing opposition or discouragement, spend time in prayer today asking God for strength to stand firm. Reflect on Christ's victory and how that impacts your confidence in Him.

DAY 3: THE FALL OF BABYLON

Read Scripture: Revelation 17:15-18
Focus Scripture: Revelation 17:16 (NASB)
*"And the ten horns which you saw, and the beast, these
will hate the harlot and will make her desolate and naked,
and will eat her flesh and will burn her up with fire."*

ANECDOTE:

Sometimes alliances built on deception and selfish ambition crumble from within. In Revelation, we see the once-powerful Babylon—the corrupt world system—turning on itself. The very forces that propped her up now become the instruments of her downfall.

EXPLANATION:

In this passage, the angel explains that the ten horns (representing kings) and the beast will ultimately turn against the woman (Babylon) and bring about her destruction. The alliance between Babylon and the powers of the world, once strong, falls apart as the beast and the kings seek to devour her.

This self-destruction highlights the temporary nature of evil. While Babylon may seem powerful and influential for a time, her end is inevitable. The powers of the world, motivated by selfish ambition and greed, ultimately consume themselves. Babylon's fall is a reminder that no worldly kingdom or power can stand against God's eternal kingdom.

God is sovereign over even the forces of evil, and He uses them to bring about His judgment. Babylon's destruction is part of God's plan to bring an end to the corrupt systems of the world and to establish His righteous reign.

APPLICATION:

The fall of Babylon challenges us to consider where we place our trust. Are we building our lives on the shifting sands of worldly power and wealth, or are we building on the solid foundation of Christ? Babylon's fall is a reminder that all worldly systems will ultimately fail, but God's kingdom will endure forever.

Are you putting your trust in things that will not last? Let this passage remind you to invest in what is eternal: your relationship with God and His kingdom. Everything else will one day fade away.

FURTHER READING:

Matthew 7:24-27, Isaiah 47:1-11, 1 John 2:17

PRAYER:

Lord, help me to place my trust in You and not in the things of this world. Remind me that all earthly powers will one day fall, but Your kingdom will last forever. Give me the wisdom to build my life on the solid foundation of Your truth. Amen.

CHALLENGE:

Take time today to reflect on where you are placing your trust. Are you relying on things that are temporary, or are you investing in God's eternal kingdom? Make a commitment to focus on what will last.

DAY 4: THE KINGS LAMENT BABYLON'S DESTRUCTION

Read Scripture: Revelation 18:9-10
Focus Scripture: Revelation 18:10 (NASB)
"Standing at a distance because of the fear of her torment, saying, 'Woe, woe, the great city, Babylon, the strong city! For in one hour your judgment has come.'"

ANECDOTE:

Imagine watching a great city, once filled with wealth and power, crumble in a matter of moments. The awe and shock of witnessing such destruction would be overwhelming. In Revelation 18, the kings of the earth lament the fall of Babylon, but their sorrow is not because of righteousness, it's because they have lost their source of wealth and power.

EXPLANATION:

The kings of the earth, who once benefited from Babylon's power and wealth, now stand at a distance, mourning her destruction. Babylon, the "strong city," seemed invincible, but in just one hour, God's judgment falls, and she is no more. The kings' lament is not out of concern for the city or its people, but for their own loss. Babylon's fall signals the end of their ability to gain wealth and power through her corrupt systems.

This passage highlights the temporary nature of worldly power and wealth. What seems strong and secure can be brought down in an instant by the hand of God. Babylon, once the center of influence and luxury, is now reduced to ruins. The kings' mourning serves as a warning to those who place their trust in material wealth and political power, for such things will not last.

APPLICATION:

The kings' lament over Babylon's destruction challenges us to consider where we find our security. Are we trusting in worldly power and wealth, or are we placing our trust in God's eternal kingdom? Babylon's fall serves as a reminder that all earthly kingdoms and systems will one day crumble, but God's kingdom will endure forever.

Are there areas in your life where you are placing too much trust in material things or worldly success? Let this passage remind you to put your hope in what will last: your relationship with God and His eternal promises.

FURTHER READING:

Psalm 62:10, Matthew 6:19-21, 1 Timothy 6:17-19

PRAYER:

Lord, help me to place my trust in You and not in the things of this world. Remind me that worldly power and wealth are temporary, but Your kingdom is eternal. Thank You for being my true source of security and hope. Amen.

CHALLENGE:

Take time today to evaluate where you are placing your trust. Are you relying too much on material wealth or success? Ask God to help you focus on what truly matters—His kingdom and His righteousness.

DAY 5: REJOICING IN HEAVEN OVER BABYLON'S FALL

Read Scripture: Revelation 18:20-24
Focus Scripture: Revelation 18:20 (NASB)
"Rejoice over her, O heaven, and you saints and apostles and prophets, because God has pronounced judgment for you against her."

ANECDOTE:

In many stories, when justice is finally served after a long period of wrongdoing, there is a sense of relief and joy. In Revelation 18, we see heaven rejoicing over the fall of Babylon, not because of destruction itself, but because God's justice has finally been carried out.

EXPLANATION:

As Babylon falls, heaven rejoices. The saints, apostles, and prophets, who have suffered under Babylon's corrupt system, now see God's judgment carried out on their behalf. This rejoicing is not over the suffering of others, but over the fact that God's justice is finally being realized. The oppression and corruption that Babylon represented have come to an end, and God's righteous rule is being established.

The fall of Babylon marks a turning point in the final events of Revelation. It signifies the end of the world's corrupt systems and the beginning of God's reign of righteousness. The rejoicing in heaven is a celebration of God's faithfulness to His people and His ultimate victory over evil.

This passage reminds us that God's justice will prevail, even when it seems delayed. For those who have suffered injustice, persecution, or oppression, Babylon's fall is a reminder that God sees, and He will act on behalf of His people.

APPLICATION:

The rejoicing in heaven over Babylon's fall challenges us to trust in God's timing and justice. While we may experience injustice or oppression in this world, we can have confidence that God's judgment is certain. He will make all things right in His time. This passage encourages us to live with the hope of God's ultimate victory, knowing that evil will not have the final word.

Are you waiting for justice in an area of your life? Let this passage remind you to trust in God's perfect timing. His justice may seem delayed, but it is never denied. Rejoice in the knowledge that God will make all things right.

FURTHER READING:

Romans 12:19, 2 Thessalonians 1:5-7, Psalm 37:7-9

PRAYER:

Lord, thank You for being a God of justice. Help me to trust in Your timing and to rejoice in the knowledge that You will make all things right. Thank You for Your faithfulness to Your people, and for the promise of Your ultimate victory over evil. Amen.

CHALLENGE:

Take time today to reflect on areas where you are waiting for justice. Commit those areas to God in prayer, and trust in His perfect timing to bring about what is right.

DAY 6: THE VOICE FROM HEAVEN

Read Scripture: Revelation 18:1-8
Focus Scripture: Revelation 18:4 (NASB)
"I heard another voice from heaven, saying, 'Come out of her, my people, so that you will not partici-pate in her sins and receive of her plagues.'"

ANECDOTE:

Imagine being in a dangerous situation and hearing a voice calling you to safety. In Revelation 18, a voice from heaven calls God's people to come out of Babylon, urging them to separate themselves from her sins and avoid sharing in her judgment.

EXPLANATION:

Before Babylon's final destruction a voice from heaven calls out to God's people, warning them to come out of her. This call is both literal and spiritual. It's an invitation to separate from the corrupt systems of the world that stand in opposition to God. Babylon represents not only a city but a way of life that is steeped in sin, greed, and immorality.

God's call to His people is clear: "Come out of her." He wants His people to be separate from the sinful practices of the world so that they do not share in the judgment that is coming. This is a call to holiness, a reminder that as followers of Christ, we are called to live differently from the world around us.

This passage echoes other biblical calls for God's people to separate themselves from sin and to live in holiness. While we live in the world, we are not to be of the world (John 17:14-16). God desires His people to be a holy nation, set apart for His purposes.

APPLICATION:

The call to come out of Babylon challenges us to examine where we may be compromising with the values of the world. Are there areas of your life where you are participating in things that are contrary to God's will? God's call is for His people to live in holiness, to be set apart for His glory.

Is there an area of your life where you need to "come out" of the world's influence? Let this passage encourage you to pursue holiness and to live in a way that reflects God's values, not the world's.

FURTHER READING:

2 Corinthians 6:17-18, 1 Peter 1:14-16, Romans 12:2

PRAYER:

Lord, help me to come out of anything that is not pleasing to You. Give me the strength to live a life of holiness, separated from the sinful influences of the world. Thank You for calling me to be Your own, and for the promise that You will protect and guide me. Amen.

CHALLENGE:

Spend time today reflecting on areas of your life where you may be influenced by the world's values. Ask God to help you "come out" of those areas and commit to living in holiness and obedience to Him.

DAY 7: THE JUDGMENT OF BABYLON COMPLETE

Read Scripture: Revelation 19:1-5
Focus Scripture: Revelation 19:2 (NASB)
"Because His judgments are true and righteous; for He has judged the great harlot who was corrupting the earth with her immorality, and He has avenged the blood of His bond-servants on her."

ANECDOTE:

There's a sense of relief and closure when justice is finally served, especially after a long period of wrongdoing. In Revelation 19, we see the final judgment of Babylon, and all of heaven rejoices, knowing that God's righteous judgment has been fully carried out.

EXPLANATION:

Revelation 19 opens with a great multitude in heaven rejoicing over the final judgment of Babylon. The phrase "Hallelujah!" rings out as the saints celebrate God's righteous judgment. Babylon, the corrupt system that opposed God and persecuted His people, has been judged, and the blood of the martyrs has been avenged.

This passage emphasizes the righteousness of God's judgment. His judgments are not arbitrary or unfair—they are true and just. Babylon's destruction is the result of her immorality, corruption, and persecution of God's people. The rejoicing in heaven reflects the satisfaction that comes from seeing God's justice fulfilled.

For believers, this passage is a reminder that God will ultimately right every wrong. The suffering and injustice we experience in this life will not last forever. God's judgment is coming, and His righteousness will prevail.

APPLICATION:

The final judgment of Babylon reminds us to live with the hope of God's justice. While we may face challenges, persecution, or injustice in this life, we can trust that God's judgment is coming and that His righteousness will prevail. This passage encourages us to persevere, knowing that God sees everything and that He will bring justice in His perfect time.

Are you facing any injustice or suffering in your life? Let this passage encourage you to trust in God's righteous judgment. He will make all things right, and His justice will prevail.

FURTHER READING:

Psalm 96:10-13, Revelation 6:10-11, Romans 12:19

PRAYER:

Lord, thank You for being a God of justice and righteousness. Help me to trust in Your timing and to persevere in faith, knowing that Your judgments are true and just. Thank You for the promise that You will right every wrong and that Your righteousness will prevail. Amen.

CHALLENGE:

Reflect on areas in your life where you may be facing injustice or difficulty. Commit those areas to God in prayer, trusting that His righteous judgment will come in His perfect timing.

WEEK 9: "BABYLON THE GREAT AND THE FALL OF EVIL"
BEYOND THE UNVEILING, GOING DEEPER

- What insights does the fall of Babylon provide about God's control over worldly powers?

- How does this chapter strengthen your hope in God's final victory over evil?

- Reflect on any ways you may rely on material or worldly things. How can you shift your focus to God?

- What lessons on humility and submission to God can you draw from Babylon's downfall?

- How does the world's judgment of Babylon contrast with God's righteous judgment?

- How does this passage encourage you to place less value on earthly possessions?

- How can you deepen your commitment to living for God's kingdom rather than the world's?

WEEK 10: THE RETURN OF THE KING

DAY 1: THE MARRIAGE SUPPER OF THE LAMB (REVELATION 19:7-10)

DAY 2: THE RIDER ON THE WHITE HORSE (REVELATION 19:11-13)

DAY 3: THE DEFEAT OF THE BEAST AND THE FALSE PROPHET (REVELATION 19:19-21)

DAY 4: THE MILLENNIAL REIGN OF CHRIST (REVELATION 20:1-6)

DAY 5: SATAN'S FINAL DEFEAT (REVELATION 20:7-10)

DAY 6: THE GREAT WHITE THRONE JUDGMENT (REVELATION 20:11-12)

DAY 7: THE SECOND DEATH (REVELATION 20:14-15)

DAY 1: THE MARRIAGE SUPPER OF THE LAMB

Read Scripture: Revelation 19:7-10
Focus Scripture: Revelation 19:7 (NASB)
"Let us rejoice and be glad and give the glory to Him, for the marriage of the Lamb has come and His bride has made herself ready."

ANECDOTE:

Think of the joy and celebration that surrounds a wedding day, where two people are united in love and commitment. In Revelation 19, we are invited to the ultimate wedding celebration—the marriage supper of the Lamb, where Christ and His church are united for all eternity.

EXPLANATION:

The marriage supper of the Lamb represents the joyful union between Christ and His bride, the church. This is the culmination of God's redemptive plan, where the faithful followers of Christ are finally united with Him in eternal fellowship. The bride has "made herself ready," clothed in fine linen, which represents the righteous acts of the saints. This beautiful imagery reminds us of the purity and holiness that Christ imparts to His church.

The celebration of this union reflects the deep, covenantal love that Christ has for His people. Just as a bridegroom prepares a place for his bride, Christ has gone to prepare a place for us (John 14:2-3), and now that preparation is complete. The marriage supper of the Lamb is a moment of great rejoicing, as the church is fully united with her Savior.

For believers, this passage is a source of hope and joy. It reminds us that we are not only followers of Christ but also His beloved bride, and one day we will be united with Him in glory. The marriage supper of the Lamb is a time of celebration, where all the sorrows and trials of this life will fade away in the presence of our loving Savior.

APPLICATION:

The marriage supper of the Lamb challenges us to live as the bride of Christ, making ourselves ready for His return. As the bride, we are called to live in purity and faithfulness, preparing ourselves for the day when we will be united with Christ. This passage invites us to rejoice in the love of Christ and to look forward with anticipation to the day when we will be with Him forever.

Are you living as the bride of Christ, preparing yourself for His return? Let this passage remind you of the joy and hope that await you as a beloved member of Christ's church, and let it inspire you to live in purity and faithfulness as you wait for His return.

FURTHER READING:

Ephesians 5:25-27, Matthew 25:1-13, John 14:1-3

PRAYER:

Lord Jesus, thank You for the promise that I am part of Your bride, the church. Help me to live in purity and faithfulness as I wait for the day when I will be united with You forever. Fill me with joy and hope as I look forward to the marriage supper of the Lamb. Amen.

CHALLENGE:

Reflect on how you are living as the bride of Christ. Are you preparing yourself for His return through purity and faithfulness? Commit today to deepening your relationship with Him and living in a way that honors your place as part of His beloved church.

DAY 2: THE RIDER ON THE WHITE HORSE

Read Scripture: Revelation 19:11-13
Focus Scripture: Revelation 19:11 (NASB)
*"And I saw heaven opened, and behold, a white horse,
and He who sat on it is called Faithful and True,
and in righteousness He judges and wages war."*

ANECDOTE:

In many stories of good versus evil, the hero arrives at just the right moment to turn the tide of battle and claim victory. In Revelation 19, we see the ultimate hero—Jesus Christ—riding on a white horse, coming in power and glory to defeat the forces of evil once and for all.

EXPLANATION:

The vision of the rider on the white horse marks the triumphant return of Christ. Jesus is depicted as "Faithful and True," a reminder that He is the ultimate fulfillment of all God's promises. His return is not as the humble servant we saw at His first coming, but as the victorious King, ready to wage war against the forces of evil.

His eyes are like a flame of fire, symbolizing His righteous judgment. He comes to wage war, not in hatred, but in righteousness, to bring an end to evil and establish His kingdom. The white horse is a symbol of purity and victory, and His return is the moment all creation has been waiting for.

For believers, this passage is a source of hope. We know that no matter how dark the world may seem, Jesus is coming again, and He will bring justice, peace, and righteousness. The rider on the white horse is the King of kings, and His victory is certain.

APPLICATION:

The rider on the white horse reminds us that Jesus is coming again, and His return will bring an end to all evil and injustice. This truth should fill us with hope and inspire us to live with an eternal perspective. While we may face trials and challenges in this world, we can have confidence that Jesus will return as the victorious King.

Are you living with the hope of Christ's return? Let this passage remind you to fix your eyes on Jesus, the Faithful and True One, and to live in anticipation of His victorious return.

FURTHER READING:

Isaiah 11:4-5, 1 Thessalonians 4:16-17, Matthew 24:30

PRAYER:

Lord Jesus, thank You for the promise of Your return. Help me to live each day with the hope and confidence that You are coming again, and that Your victory is certain. Strengthen my faith and fill me with the joy of knowing that You are the King of kings and Lord of lords. Amen.

CHALLENGE:

Take time today to reflect on the hope of Christ's return. How does this truth impact the way you live your life? Ask God to help you live with an eternal perspective, keeping your focus on His coming kingdom.

DAY 3: THE DEFEAT OF THE BEAST AND THE FALSE PROPHET

Read Scripture: Revelation 19:19-21
Focus Scripture: Revelation 19:20 (NASB)
"And the beast was seized, and with him the false prophet who performed the signs in his presence, by which he deceived those who had received the mark of the beast and those who worshiped his image; these two were thrown alive into the lake of fire which burns with brimstone."

ANECDOTE:

In a dramatic courtroom scene, the guilty are brought to justice, and the deceptive schemes of evil are exposed for all to see. In Revelation 19, the final defeat of the beast and the false prophet is a moment of ultimate justice, where the forces of deception and rebellion against God are forever vanquished.

EXPLANATION:

The defeat of the beast and the false prophet marks the culmination of their rebellion against God. These two figures represent the forces of evil that have deceived the nations, leading people away from the truth of God. Throughout the tribulation, the beast and the false prophet have wielded power and influence, deceiving many with signs and wonders. But now, their reign of deception comes to an end.

The beast and the false prophet are captured and thrown alive into the lake of fire, a place of eternal punishment. This is a reminder of the finality of God's judgment. Their defeat is swift and complete, and they are no longer able to deceive or harm God's people.

For believers, this passage brings great hope. It reminds us that evil will not have the last word. God's justice will prevail. The defeat of the beast and the false prophet is a powerful reminder that no matter how strong the forces of evil may seem, they are ultimately powerless before the authority of Christ.

APPLICATION:

The defeat of the beast and the false prophet challenges us to remain faithful to Christ, even in the face of deception and opposition. The world may offer many false promises and temptations, but only Christ can offer true life and victory. This passage reminds us to stand firm in our faith, knowing that the forces of evil will ultimately be defeated.

Are you facing any forms of deception or temptation in your life? Let this passage encourage you to stand firm in your faith, trusting that Christ has already won the victory over all the forces of evil.

FURTHER READING:

2 Thessalonians 2:8-10, 1 John 4:1-6, John 16:33

PRAYER:

Lord, thank You for the promise that evil will be defeated and that You are victorious. Help me to stand firm in my faith, resisting the deception and temptations of this world. Strengthen my heart to trust in Your victory and to live each day with confidence in Your power. Amen.

CHALLENGE:

Identify any areas in your life where you may be tempted by deception or false promises. Commit those areas to God in prayer, asking Him to help you remain faithful and stand firm in the truth of His Word.

DAY 4: THE MILLENNIAL REIGN OF CHRIST

Read Scripture: Revelation 20:1-6
Focus Scripture: Revelation 20:4 (NASB)
"Then I saw thrones, and they sat on them, and judgment was given to them. And I saw the souls of those who had been beheaded because of their testimony of Jesus... and they came to life and reigned with Christ for a thousand years."

ANECDOTE:

Think of a time when peace finally arrived after a long period of conflict. In Revelation 20, we are given a glimpse of the millennial reign of Christ, a time of peace and righteousness where Christ reigns as King and His faithful followers share in His victory.

EXPLANATION:

The millennial reign of Christ marks a thousand-year period where Jesus reigns on earth as King. During this time, Satan is bound, unable to deceive the nations, and the saints reign with Christ. Those who were faithful to Christ, even to the point of martyrdom, are resurrected and share in this reign.

This period is a time of peace, justice, and righteousness, where Christ's rule is fully realized. The millennial reign is a fulfillment of God's promises to His people, where His kingdom is established on earth, and those who have been faithful share in the blessings of His reign.

For believers, this passage is a reminder that our faithfulness to Christ will be rewarded. While we may face challenges, opposition, and even persecution in this life, we can have confidence that we will reign with Christ in His coming kingdom.

APPLICATION:

The millennial reign of Christ challenges us to live with the hope of His coming kingdom. While we may face trials and difficulties in this life, we can trust that our faithfulness to Christ will be rewarded. This passage encourages us to persevere in our faith, knowing that we will share in Christ's reign.

Are you living with the hope of Christ's kingdom? Let this passage remind you to persevere in your faith, trusting that your reward is secure in Christ's coming reign.

FURTHER READING:

Isaiah 2:2-4, Matthew 19:28-29, 2 Timothy 2:12

PRAYER:

Lord, thank You for the promise of Your coming kingdom. Help me to live each day with the hope of reigning with You, and to persevere in my faith, even in the face of challenges. Thank You for the assurance that my reward is secure in You. Amen.

CHALLENGE:

Reflect on how the promise of Christ's millennial reign affects the way you live today. Ask God to help you live with hope and confidence, knowing that you will share in His kingdom.

DAY 5: SATAN'S FINAL DEFEAT

Read Scripture: Revelation 20:7-10
Focus Scripture: Revelation 20:10 (NASB)
*"And the devil who deceived them was thrown into the lake of
fire and brimstone, where the beast and the false prophet are also;
and they will be tormented day and night forever and ever."*

ANECDOTE:

Think of the moment when the villain in a story is finally defeated,
and all the damage they've done is brought to an end. In Revelation 20,
we see the ultimate defeat of Satan—the one who has deceived the nations—being cast into the lake of fire, never to torment or deceive again.

EXPLANATION:

Satan's final defeat comes after the millennial reign of Christ. Though
he is released for a short time to deceive the nations once again, his rebellion is short-lived. Fire comes down from heaven to devour those who
have been deceived, and Satan is cast into the lake of fire, where he will
be tormented forever.

This moment marks the end of Satan's influence and the end of evil's
power in the world. No longer will he be able to deceive or harm humanity. The finality of his defeat is a reminder that evil will not have the last
word and God's victory is complete.

For believers, this passage brings hope and assurance. It reminds us
that while we may face spiritual battles now, the day is coming when Satan will be defeated forever, and we will live in the full presence of God's
peace and righteousness.

APPLICATION:

Satan's final defeat encourages us to remain steadfast in our faith, knowing that the enemy's power is temporary. While we may experience spiritual warfare in this life, we can have confidence that Satan's defeat is certain. This passage calls us to trust in God's victory and to live with the assurance that evil will not prevail.

Are you facing spiritual challenges or feeling discouraged by the power of evil in the world? Let this passage remind you that Satan's defeat is sure, and Christ's victory is complete. Stand firm in your faith, knowing that the battle has already been won.

FURTHER READING:

Romans 16:20, Ephesians 6:10-12, 1 Peter 5:8-9

PRAYER:

Lord, thank You for the promise of Satan's final defeat. Help me to stand firm in my faith, even when I face spiritual battles. Remind me that Your victory is already won, and that Satan's power is temporary. Strengthen me to live in confidence and peace, knowing that You are victorious. Amen.

CHALLENGE:

Reflect on any spiritual challenges you are facing and surrender them to God, trusting in His victory. Ask God to strengthen your faith and help you stand firm in the face of spiritual warfare.

DAY 6: THE GREAT WHITE THRONE JUDGMENT

Read Scripture: Revelation 20:11-12
Focus Scripture: Revelation 20:12 (NASB)
"And I saw the dead, the great and the small, standing before the throne, and books were opened; and another book was opened, which is the book of life; and the dead were judged from the things which were written in the books, according to their deeds."

ANECDOTE:

Imagine standing in a courtroom, knowing that everything you've ever done will be laid bare for judgment. In Revelation 20, we are given a glimpse of the Great White Throne Judgment, where all of humanity will stand before God to be judged according to what is written in the books.

EXPLANATION:

The Great White Throne Judgment is the final judgment, where all the dead—both great and small—stand before God to be judged. The books are opened, and each person is judged according to their deeds. Another book, the book of life, is also opened, and those whose names are found in the book of life will be spared from eternal punishment.

This moment emphasizes the seriousness of God's judgment. No one can escape it, and every deed will be accounted for. The distinction between those who are judged by their deeds and those who are in the book of life is significant. Those who are not found in the book of life will face eternal separation from God.

For believers, this passage is both sobering and reassuring. While we know that judgment is real, we also have the assurance that through faith in Christ, our names are written in the book of life. Our salvation is secure, and we will not face the punishment that comes with being judged by our deeds alone.

APPLICATION:

The Great White Throne Judgment challenges us to live in light of eternity, knowing that we will one day stand before God. This passage reminds us of the seriousness of sin and the importance of living a life that honors God. At the same time it gives us hope, knowing that through Christ, we have been spared from judgment.

Are you living with the awareness of God's judgment? Let this passage remind you to live a life that reflects your faith in Christ, knowing that your salvation is secure in Him.

FURTHER READING:

Hebrews 9:27-28, Matthew 25:31-34, John 5:24

PRAYER:

Lord, thank You for the assurance that my name is written in the book of life. Help me to live each day with the awareness of Your judgment and the desire to honor You with my life. Thank You for the promise of eternal life through faith in Christ. Amen.

CHALLENGE:

Take time today to reflect on the seriousness of God's judgment and the assurance you have through faith in Christ. Commit to living in a way that honors God, knowing that your salvation is secure in Him.

DAY 7: THE SECOND DEATH

Read Scripture: Revelation 20:14-15
Focus Scripture: Revelation 20:14 (NASB)
"Then death and Hades were thrown into the lake of fire. This is the second death, the lake of fire."

ANECDOTE:

The fear of death is something that many people wrestle with, but in Revelation 20, we see that even death itself will one day be destroyed. The "second death" represents eternal separation from God, but for believers, this is something we have been spared from through Christ.

EXPLANATION:

The second death refers to the lake of fire, a place of eternal punishment for those who are not found in the book of life. Death and Hades, which have held power over humanity since the fall, are thrown into the lake of fire, marking the end of their reign. For those who have rejected Christ, the second death is a reality, a separation from God for all eternity.

However for believers, the second death has no power over us. Through faith in Christ, we are promised eternal life, and we will never face the second death. This passage is a reminder of both the seriousness of rejecting God and the incredible hope we have in Christ.

For those who trust in Jesus, the fear of death is replaced with the hope of eternal life. Death, which once seemed like the ultimate enemy, is now defeated through Christ's victory.

APPLICATION:

The second death reminds us of the urgency of the gospel and the importance of sharing the hope of eternal life with others. While we have been spared from the second death through faith in Christ, many still face the reality of eternal separation from God. This passage challenges us to share the message of salvation with those who do not yet know Christ.

Are you living with the hope of eternal life? Let this passage remind you of the victory you have in Christ and inspire you to share the gospel with others so that they too can be spared from the second death.

FURTHER READING:

1 Corinthians 15:54-57, John 11:25-26, Romans 6:23

PRAYER:

Lord, thank You for the promise of eternal life and for sparing me from the second death. Help me to live with the hope of Your victory over death, and give me the courage to share this hope with others. Thank You for the assurance that death has been defeated, and that I have eternal life in You. Amen.

CHALLENGE:

Reflect on the reality of eternal life and the victory you have in Christ. Take time this week to share the message of salvation with someone who needs to hear it, offering them the hope of eternal life through Jesus.

WEEK 10: "THE RETURN OF THE KING"

BEYOND THE UNVEILING, GOING DEEPER

- How does the vision of Christ's return inspire you to live with greater expectation and readiness?

- What does the marriage supper of the Lamb symbolize to you personally?

- Reflect on how the return of Christ fulfills God's promises. How does this strengthen your faith?

- How does the imagery of Christ as a conquering King impact your view of Him?

- What does it mean for you to prepare for the return of the King?

- How does the promise of final victory affect your perspective on current challenges?

- How can you actively prepare your heart and life for Christ's return?

WEEK 11: THE NEW HEAVEN, NEW EARTH, AND NEW JERUSALEM

Day 1: A New Heaven and a New Earth (Revelation 21:1-2)

Day 2: God Dwelling with His People (Revelation 21:3-4)

Day 3: All Things Made New (Revelation 21:5-8)

Day 4: The Glory of the New Jerusalem (Revelation 21:9-11)

Day 5: The Radiance of God's Presence (Revelation 21:22-23)

Day 6: No More Night (Revelation 21:24-27)

Day 7: The River of Life (Revelation 22:1-2)

DAY 1: A NEW HEAVEN AND A NEW EARTH

Read Scripture: Revelation 21:1-2
Focus Scripture: Revelation 21:1 (NASB)
"Then I saw a new heaven and a new earth; for the first heaven and the first earth passed away, and there is no longer any sea."

ANECDOTE:

Imagine standing on the shore of the ocean, gazing out at its vastness. Now imagine a world without oceans, a world completely new and transformed. In Revelation 21, John sees a vision of a new heaven and a new earth, unlike anything we have ever known. The old order of things has passed away, and God is creating something entirely new.

EXPLANATION:

The vision of the new heaven and new earth is one of the most beautiful and hopeful passages in Revelation. The first heaven and earth, which have been corrupted by sin and decay, are no more. In their place, God creates a new heaven and earth, a perfect and restored creation where sin, death, and suffering have no place.

The absence of the sea may symbolize the removal of chaos and danger, as the sea often represented turmoil in ancient thought. This new creation is one of perfect peace, where nothing separates God's people from His presence.

This passage marks the beginning of eternity in the new creation, where God's people will dwell with Him forever. The hope of the new heaven and new earth is a promise of complete restoration—where all things will be made new, and the sorrows of the past will be wiped away.

APPLICATION:

The vision of the new heaven and new earth invites us to live with hope, knowing that no matter how difficult life may be now, God is preparing something far greater for His people. This passage encourages us to fix our eyes on eternity and to live with the assurance that God will one day make all things new.

Are you holding on to the hope of the new heaven and new earth? Let this passage remind you that no matter what you face in this world, God has promised a future of restoration and peace.

FURTHER READING:

Isaiah 65:17-18, 2 Peter 3:13, Romans 8:18-21

PRAYER:

Lord, thank You for the promise of a new heaven and a new earth. Help me to live with hope, knowing that You will one day restore all things and make all things new. Give me the strength to persevere in faith, trusting in Your eternal promises. Amen.

CHALLENGE:

Take time today to reflect on the promise of the new heaven and new earth. How does this truth impact the way you live today? Ask God to help you live with the hope and assurance of His coming restoration.

DAY 2: GOD DWELLING WITH HIS PEOPLE

Read Scripture: Revelation 21:3-4
Focus Scripture: Revelation 21:3 (NASB)
*"And I heard a loud voice from the throne, saying, 'Behold, the tab-
ernacle of God is among men, and He will dwell among them, and
they shall be His people, and God Himself will be among them.'"*

ANECDOTE:

Imagine being reunited with a loved one after a long time apart. The
joy of being together again, face to face, is overwhelming. In Revelation
21, we are given the ultimate promise of reunion—God Himself will
dwell with His people, and we will be in His presence forever.

EXPLANATION:

The promise of God dwelling with His people is one of the most
profound and comforting promises in Scripture. In the new creation,
God will no longer be distant or unseen; He will be fully present with
His people, and we will experience the joy of His presence forever. The
word "tabernacle" recalls the Old Testament, where God dwelled among
His people in the tabernacle, a temporary dwelling. But now, in the new
heaven and new earth, God's presence will be permanent and complete.

This passage also brings comfort to those who have experienced pain
and loss in this life. God will wipe away every tear, and death, mourning,
crying, and pain will be no more. The brokenness of this world will be
healed, and we will live in perfect fellowship with God.

For believers, this passage is a source of great hope. It reminds us
that the ultimate joy of eternity is not just the absence of pain but the
presence of God Himself. We will dwell with Him, and He will dwell
with us forever.

APPLICATION:

The promise of God dwelling with His people invites us to live with the anticipation of being in His presence forever. While we may face trials and sorrows in this life, we can have confidence that God will one day wipe away every tear and bring us into perfect fellowship with Him. This passage encourages us to persevere in faith, knowing that our future with God is secure.

Are you living with the hope of dwelling with God in eternity? Let this passage remind you of the joy and peace that await you in the presence of God, and let it inspire you to live each day in anticipation of that glorious reunion.

FURTHER READING:

John 14:1-3, 1 Corinthians 13:12, Ezekiel 37:27

PRAYER:

Lord, thank You for the promise that I will one day dwell with You forever. Help me to live with the hope of Your presence and to persevere in faith, knowing that every tear will be wiped away. Thank You for the comfort of Your love and the assurance of eternal life with You. Amen.

CHALLENGE:

Reflect on the promise of dwelling with God in eternity. How does this truth comfort you in times of difficulty? Spend time in prayer, thanking God for the hope of His presence and asking Him to help you live with that hope each day.

DAY 3: ALL THINGS MADE NEW

Read Scripture: Revelation 21:5-8
Focus Scripture: Revelation 21:5 (NASB)
*"And He who sits on the throne said, 'Behold, I
am making all things new.' And He said, 'Write,
for these words are faithful and true.'"*

ANECDOTE:

Think of the excitement of starting something new—a fresh beginning, a clean slate. In Revelation 21 God declares that He is making all things new, bringing hope and renewal to a world that has been broken by sin and suffering.

EXPLANATION:

In this passage, God Himself speaks from the throne, declaring that He is making all things new. This is the ultimate promise of renewal and restoration. Everything that has been marred by sin—creation, humanity, relationships—will be made new. The old order of things, with its pain, suffering, and death, will be replaced by God's perfect order of peace and life.

God's declaration is followed by the assurance that these words are "faithful and true." This reminds us that we can trust in God's promises. The new heaven and new earth are not just wishful thinking; they are a reality that God has prepared for His people.

This passage also includes a warning for those who reject God's offer of salvation. Those who remain in rebellion against God will not inherit this new creation but will face the "second death," eternal separation from God. The contrast between the blessings of the new creation and the consequences of rejecting God's grace is stark.

APPLICATION:

The promise that God is making all things new invites us to live with hope and expectancy, knowing that the brokenness of this world will one day be healed. This passage challenges us to trust in God's promises and to live in a way that reflects the hope of renewal and restoration.

Are you trusting in God's promise to make all things new? Let this passage remind you that no matter how broken this world may seem, God is at work, bringing about His perfect plan of renewal.

FURTHER READING:

Isaiah 43:18-19, 2 Corinthians 5:17, Romans 8:22-23

PRAYER:

Lord, thank You for the promise that You are making all things new. Help me to trust in Your faithful and true words and to live with the hope of renewal and restoration. Thank You for the assurance that no matter how broken this world may be, You are at work, bringing about Your perfect plan. Amen.

CHALLENGE:

Take time today to reflect on how God is making all things new. Are there areas of your life where you need to trust in His promise of renewal?

DAY 4: THE GLORY OF THE NEW JERUSALEM

Read Scripture: Revelation 21:9-11
Focus Scripture: Revelation 21:11 (NASB)
*"Her brilliance was like a very costly stone,
as a stone of crystal-clear jasper."*

ANECDOTE:

Have you ever seen a city skyline illuminated at night, with lights reflecting off the buildings, creating a breathtaking scene of beauty? Now imagine a city whose glory doesn't come from lights or architecture but from the very presence of God. This is the vision of the New Jerusalem in Revelation 21, a city of unimaginable glory and beauty.

EXPLANATION:

In this passage, one of the angels invites John to see the "bride, the wife of the Lamb," which represents the New Jerusalem, the eternal dwelling place of God's people. The city is described as having a brilliance like that of a precious stone, clear as crystal. This imagery highlights the purity, beauty, and radiance of the New Jerusalem, a city that reflects the glory of God.

The New Jerusalem is not just a physical city but a symbol of the eternal dwelling place of God's people. It is the fulfillment of God's promises to restore His creation and to bring His people into perfect fellowship with Him. The brilliance of the city reflects the purity and holiness of God's presence, where no sin or impurity can dwell.

This passage gives us a glimpse of the glory that awaits believers in eternity. The New Jerusalem is a place of beauty, peace, and joy, where God's people will dwell with Him forever. The vision of this city reminds us of the hope we have in Christ and the glory that awaits us in the new creation.

APPLICATION:

The glory of the New Jerusalem challenges us to live with an eternal perspective, knowing that the beauty and joy of God's presence await us. While we may experience brokenness and pain in this world, we can have confidence that our eternal home will be a place of unimaginable glory and peace. This passage encourages us to persevere in faith, knowing that the trials of this life are temporary compared to the eternal glory of the New Jerusalem.

Are you living with the hope of the New Jerusalem in mind? Let this passage remind you of the beauty and glory that await you in God's presence, and let it inspire you to live with an eternal perspective.

FURTHER READING:

Hebrews 11:10, Isaiah 60:19-20, John 14:1-3

PRAYER:

Lord, thank You for the promise of the New Jerusalem, a place of beauty and glory where I will dwell with You forever. Help me to live with the hope of eternity in mind, and to persevere in faith, knowing that the trials of this life are temporary compared to the glory that awaits me. Amen.

CHALLENGE:

Spend time reflecting on the glory of the New Jerusalem. How does the promise of this eternal city impact the way you live today? Ask God to help you live with an eternal perspective, focusing on the hope of what is to come.

DAY 5: THE RADIANCE OF GOD'S PRESENCE

Read Scripture: Revelation 21:22-23
Focus Scripture: Revelation 21:23 (NASB)
*"And the city has no need of the sun or of the moon to shine on it,
for the glory of God has illumined it, and its lamp is the Lamb."*

ANECDOTE:

Have you ever watched a sunrise light up the world, filling everything with warmth and brilliance? In the New Jerusalem, there will be no need for the sun or moon because the very presence of God will radiate light and glory throughout the city. The Lamb, Jesus Christ, will be its eternal source of light.

EXPLANATION:

In this passage, we are given a profound truth about the New Jerusalem: the city will not need any external source of light. The glory of God will provide all the light needed, and the Lamb, Jesus Christ, will be its lamp. This imagery reveals the fullness of God's presence in the city, where His glory will shine continuously, bringing peace, joy, and holiness to His people.

The fact that God Himself is the light of the city symbolizes the complete and perfect fellowship that believers will enjoy with Him. There will be no more darkness, no more separation from God's presence because His glory will permeate everything. The Lamb's radiance speaks of Christ's role as the light of the world, and in eternity, His light will never fade.

For believers, this passage reminds us that Jesus is the light of our lives, both now and forever. The radiance of God's presence in the New Jerusalem is a promise that we will dwell in the fullness of His glory for all eternity.

APPLICATION:

The radiance of God's presence challenges us to live in the light of Christ now, knowing that His presence will one day fill all of creation. As believers, we are called to walk in the light, reflecting the love and holiness of Christ in our lives. This passage invites us to live in the assurance that God's presence will one day banish all darkness and bring perfect peace.

Are you walking in the light of Christ? Let this passage remind you of the joy and hope of dwelling in God's eternal presence, and let it inspire you to live as a light in the world today.

FURTHER READING:

John 8:12, 1 John 1:5-7, Isaiah 60:19-20

PRAYER:

Lord, thank You for being the light of the world and for the promise that Your presence will one day fill all of creation. Help me to walk in Your light now, reflecting Your love and holiness in my life. Thank You for the hope of dwelling in Your eternal presence, where there will be no more darkness. Amen.

CHALLENGE:

Spend time today reflecting on how you can walk in the light of Christ. Are there areas of your life where you need to surrender to His light? Commit to living as a reflection of His love and holiness, knowing that His light will one day fill all of creation.

DAY 6: NO MORE NIGHT

Read Scripture: Revelation 21:24-27
Focus Scripture: Revelation 21:25 (NASB)
"In the daytime (for there will be no night there) its gates will never be closed."

ANECDOTE:

Have you ever been afraid of the dark? For many, night brings uncertainty and fear. But in the New Jerusalem, there will be no more night. The gates of the city will remain open because there will be no need for fear or darkness. The light of God will shine forever.

EXPLANATION:

In the New Jerusalem, night will no longer exist. This is more than just a physical reality; it represents the end of all that darkness symbolizes: fear, evil, separation from God. The gates of the city will never close, symbolizing perfect security, peace, and openness. There will be no need for protection because all threats will be gone, and God's people will live in complete safety and joy.

The absence of night also points to the continual presence of God's light. His glory will shine without interruption, and His people will live in the fullness of His peace. This is a place where nothing impure can enter, where all is holy and good.

For believers, this passage is a beautiful promise of the peace and security that await us in eternity. There will be no more fear, no more danger, no more separation from God—only the joy of living in His presence forever.

APPLICATION:

The promise of no more night invites us to live without fear, knowing that God is our eternal protector. While we may face darkness in this world, we can trust that in God's presence, there is perfect security and peace. This passage challenges us to place our trust in God's protection and to live in the confidence that He will bring us into His eternal light.

Are you trusting in God's protection, or are there areas of your life where fear has crept in? Let this passage remind you that in God's presence, there is no more night, no more fear or uncertainty, only the peace of His eternal light.

FURTHER READING:

Psalm 27:1, Isaiah 60:18-19, John 1:5

PRAYER:

Lord, thank You for the promise that in Your eternal kingdom, there will be no more night. Help me to live without fear, trusting in Your protection and knowing that Your light will shine forever. Thank You for the peace and security that come from being in Your presence. Amen.

CHALLENGE:

Reflect on areas in your life where fear or uncertainty may have taken hold. Surrender those areas to God, trusting that His light will banish all darkness and that His protection is secure.

DAY 7: THE RIVER OF LIFE

Read Scripture: Revelation 22:1-2
Focus Scripture: Revelation 22:1 (NASB)
"Then he showed me a river of the water of life, clear as crystal, coming from the throne of God and of the Lamb."

ANECDOTE:

Think of a beautiful river, flowing with clear, life-giving water. In Revelation 22, John is shown the river of the water of life, flowing from the throne of God and of the Lamb. This river symbolizes the eternal life and nourishment that God provides for His people.

EXPLANATION:

The river of life flows from the very throne of God and of the Lamb, symbolizing the source of all life and blessing in the new creation. This crystal-clear river represents the life-giving presence of God, which nourishes and sustains His people for all eternity. The imagery recalls the Garden of Eden, where a river flowed through paradise, but now it is fulfilled in the eternal paradise of the New Jerusalem.

Along the banks of the river is the tree of life, bearing fruit and providing healing for the nations. This is a picture of abundance, health, and eternal life. The curse that once plagued creation is now lifted, and God's people will experience the fullness of life in His presence forever.

For believers, this passage is a reminder of the eternal life we have in Christ. The river of life is a symbol of the continual, unending flow of God's grace, love, and provision for His people. In eternity, we will never hunger or thirst again, for we will be fully satisfied in God's presence.

APPLICATION:

The river of life challenges us to seek the true source of life—God Himself. While the world offers many things that promise satisfaction, only the life-giving presence of God can truly nourish and sustain us. This passage invites us to drink deeply from the water of life, knowing that in Christ, we have everything we need for eternal life.

Are you drinking from the water of life, or are you seeking satisfaction in other things? Let this passage remind you that true life comes from God alone, and let it inspire you to seek Him as your source of life and joy.

FURTHER READING:

John 4:14, Psalm 46:4, Ezekiel 47:1-12

PRAYER:

Lord, thank You for the promise of the river of life, flowing from Your throne. Help me to seek You as the true source of life and to drink deeply from Your presence. Thank You for the eternal life You have given me through Christ, and for the promise of being fully satisfied in You forever. Amen.

CHALLENGE:

Reflect on where you are seeking satisfaction and life. Are you turning to God as your source of life, or are you relying on other things? Commit today to drink from the water of life, seeking God as your ultimate source of nourishment and joy.

WEEK 11: "THE NEW HEAVEN, NEW EARTH, AND NEW JERUSALEM"

BEYOND THE UNVEILING, GOING DEEPER

- What hope does the promise of a new heaven and new earth bring to you?

- Reflect on the significance of God dwelling with His people. How does this deepen your relationship with Him?

- How does the vision of the New Jerusalem inspire your understanding of eternity?

- What aspects of the New Jerusalem are most meaningful to you, and why?

- How can this vision of eternity shape your life today?

- How does knowing there will be "no more night" bring you comfort and peace?

- How can you live each day with a renewed focus on your eternal home?

WEEK 12: THE FINAL INVITATION AND WARNING

DAY 1: THE ALPHA AND THE OMEGA
(REVELATION 22:12-13)

DAY 2: BLESSED ARE THOSE
WHO WASH THEIR ROBES
(REVELATION 22:14-15)

DAY 3: OUTSIDE ARE THE DOGS
(REVELATION 22:15)

DAY 4: THE SPIRIT AND THE BRIDE SAY,
'COME' (REVELATION 22:17)

DAY 5: THE WARNING AGAINST
ADDING OR TAKING AWAY
(REVELATION 22:18-19)

DAY 6: THE PROMISE OF CHRIST'S
RETURN (REVELATION 22:20)

DAY 7: COME, LORD JESUS
(REVELATION 22:21)

DAY 1: THE ALPHA AND THE OMEGA

Read Scripture: Revelation 22:12-13
Focus Scripture: Revelation 22:13 (NASB)
*"I am the Alpha and the Omega, the first and
the last, the beginning and the end."*

ANECDOTE:

Think about a journey that begins at one point and ends at another. No matter how long or winding the road, every journey has a beginning and an end. In Revelation 22, Jesus declares Himself as the Alpha and the Omega—the beginning and the end—reminding us that He is Lord over all of history, from start to finish.

EXPLANATION:

In this passage, Jesus identifies Himself as the Alpha and the Omega, using the first and last letters of the Greek alphabet to signify His eternal nature. He is the beginning and the end, the One who was before all things and the One who will bring all things to their final completion. This declaration is a reminder of Christ's sovereignty over all of history and His ultimate authority over creation.

As the Alpha, Jesus was present at creation, the One through whom all things were made (John 1:1-3). As the Omega, He will be there at the end, bringing history to its final fulfillment in God's eternal kingdom. This gives us great confidence as believers; no matter what happens in the world, we know that Jesus is in control, from beginning to end.

For believers, this passage is a source of comfort and assurance. We can trust that Jesus holds all of time and history in His hands, and He will bring about His perfect plan. He is the One who began our story, and He will be there to see it through to completion.

APPLICATION:

The declaration that Jesus is the Alpha and the Omega challenges us to trust in His sovereignty over our lives. Just as He is Lord over the beginning and the end of all things, He is Lord over every moment of our lives. This passage encourages us to surrender our plans and trust that Jesus is guiding our journey from start to finish.

Are you trusting Jesus as the Alpha and Omega of your life? Let this passage remind you that He is in control of your past, present, and future, and that He will bring about His perfect plan in your life.

FURTHER READING:

Isaiah 44:6, Hebrews 12:2, Colossians 1:16-17

PRAYER:

Lord Jesus, thank You for being the Alpha and the Omega, the One who holds all of history in Your hands. Help me to trust You as the Lord of my life, knowing that You are in control from beginning to end. Thank You for the assurance that You will complete the good work You have begun in me. Amen.

CHALLENGE:

Spend time today reflecting on how Jesus is the Alpha and Omega of your life. Are there areas where you are struggling to trust Him? Surrender those areas to Him, knowing that He is guiding your journey from start to finish.

DAY 2: BLESSED ARE THOSE WHO WASH THEIR ROBES

Read Scripture: Revelation 22:14-15
Focus Scripture: Revelation 22:14 (NASB)
"Blessed are those who wash their robes, so that they may have the right to the tree of life, and may enter by the gates into the city."

ANECDOTE:

Imagine being invited to a grand banquet, but before entering, you're told that your clothes must be clean and spotless. In Revelation 22, we are given a similar picture of those who enter the New Jerusalem. Only those who have "washed their robes" have the right to enter and partake of the tree of life.

EXPLANATION:

The imagery of "washing robes" in this passage symbolizes the cleansing that comes through the blood of Christ. Those who have washed their robes are those who have placed their faith in Jesus and have been cleansed from sin by His sacrifice. This cleansing grants them access to the tree of life and entry into the eternal city: the New Jerusalem.

The tree of life, which was present in the Garden of Eden, now reappears in the New Jerusalem, symbolizing eternal life with God. Only those who have been cleansed by Christ have the right to partake of this life and to enter the gates of the city.

This passage also serves as a reminder that not everyone will enter the city. Those who remain outside (those who continue in sin and rebellion against God) will not have access to the blessings of eternal life. The contrast between those inside the city and those outside highlights the importance of accepting Christ's offer of salvation.

APPLICATION:

The blessing of those who have washed their robes challenges us to examine whether we have truly placed our faith in Christ. Are we trusting in His sacrifice for the cleansing of our sins? This passage invites us to rest in the assurance of our salvation, knowing that through Christ, we have the right to eternal life.

Have you washed your robes in the blood of Christ? Let this passage remind you of the blessing and hope that come through faith in Jesus, and let it encourage you to share this hope with others.

FURTHER READING:

Isaiah 1:18, Revelation 7:14, Titus 3:5-7

PRAYER:

Lord, thank You for the cleansing that comes through Your sacrifice. Help me to trust fully in You and to rest in the assurance that through Your blood, I have the right to eternal life. Thank You for the blessing of being able to enter the city and partake of the tree of life. Amen.

CHALLENGE:

Reflect on the significance of having "washed your robes" in Christ. How does this assurance of salvation impact your daily life? Take time today to thank God for the gift of eternal life and to share this hope with someone who needs to hear it.

DAY 3: OUTSIDE ARE THE DOGS

Read Scripture: Revelation 22:15
Focus Scripture: Revelation 22:15 (NASB)
"Outside are the dogs and the sorcerers and the immoral persons and the murderers and the idolaters, and everyone who loves and practices lying."

ANECDOTE:

Imagine standing at the gates of a beautiful city, but knowing you're not allowed in because of something that separates you from the residents. In Revelation 22, we see a solemn warning about those who remain outside the city: those who have rejected God's offer of salvation and chosen to continue in sin.

EXPLANATION:

The term "dogs" in this passage is used to describe those who are impure and unclean, spiritually speaking. Along with the "dogs" are listed sorcerers, immoral persons, murderers, idolaters, and liars. These are individuals who have rejected God's grace and continue in sinful rebellion. They are excluded from the New Jerusalem, unable to enter into the blessings of eternal life.

This passage serves as a stark reminder of the consequences of rejecting God's offer of salvation. Those who persist in sin and refuse to repent will not have access to the tree of life or the gates of the eternal city. Their place is outside, separated from God and His people.

For believers, this passage is a call to remain faithful and to live in holiness. It also serves as a reminder of the urgency of sharing the gospel with others, so that they too may come to repentance and enter into the blessings of eternal life.

APPLICATION:

The warning about those outside the city challenges us to examine our own lives and to remain vigilant against sin. Are we living in a way that reflects our identity as God's people, or are we allowing sin to creep in? This passage also compels us to share the message of salvation with those who are still outside, so that they may come to know Christ and enter into His kingdom.

Are there areas of your life where you need to repent and turn back to God? Let this passage remind you of the importance of living in holiness and the urgency of sharing the gospel with others.

FURTHER READING:

1 Corinthians 6:9-11, Galatians 5:19-21, Matthew 7:21-23

PRAYER:

Lord, help me to live in a way that reflects my identity as Your child. Keep me from the sins that separate me from You, and give me the strength to walk in holiness. Thank You for the gift of salvation, and help me to share that gift with others who need to hear it. Amen.

CHALLENGE:

Take time today to reflect on areas of your life where you may need to turn back to God. Confess any sins that have crept in and commit to living in holiness.

DAY 4: THE SPIRIT AND THE BRIDE SAY, 'COME'

Read Scripture: Revelation 22:17
Focus Scripture: Revelation 22:17 (NASB)
"The Spirit and the bride say, 'Come.' And let the one who hears say, 'Come.' And let the one who is thirsty come; let the one who wishes take the water of life without cost."

ANECDOTE:

Have you ever been invited to a celebration or event that you eagerly anticipated, knowing it would be a time of joy and fellowship? In Revelation 22, we are given the ultimate invitation—the Spirit and the bride invite all who are thirsty to come and take the water of life. This is an open invitation to eternal life and fellowship with God.

EXPLANATION:

This passage contains one of the most beautiful invitations in Scripture. The Holy Spirit and the bride, which represents the church, issue a call for all who are thirsty to come and receive the water of life. The invitation is extended to everyone who recognizes their need for salvation, offering them the gift of eternal life freely and without cost.

The water of life symbolizes the eternal life that God offers to all who come to Him through faith in Jesus Christ. It is a gift that cannot be earned or bought. It is freely given by God's grace. The call to "come" is a reminder that salvation is available to all who are willing to accept it.

This passage also emphasizes the role of the church (the bride) in extending the invitation to others. As believers, we are called to echo the Spirit's invitation, inviting others to come to Christ and receive the water of life. This is not only a call to experience God's grace ourselves but to share that grace with others.

APPLICATION:

The invitation to come and take the water of life challenges us to consider whether we have responded to God's call. Have we come to Christ and received the free gift of salvation, or are we still trying to find satisfaction in other things? This passage also encourages us to extend the invitation to others, sharing the good news of salvation with those who are spiritually thirsty.

Have you responded to the invitation to come to Christ? Let this passage remind you of the free gift of eternal life, and let it inspire you to share that invitation with others who are in need of God's grace.

FURTHER READING:

Isaiah 55:1-3, John 7:37-38, Matthew 11:28-30

PRAYER:

Lord, thank You for the invitation to come and receive the water of life. Help me to recognize my need for You and to come to You each day for the life and grace that only You can give. Use me to extend Your invitation to others, that they too may come and experience Your love and salvation. Amen.

CHALLENGE:

Reflect on whether you've fully responded to God's invitation to come and take the water of life. If not, take time today to come to Him in faith and surrender. Consider sharing this invitation with someone in your life who is spiritually thirsty and in need of God's grace.

DAY 5: THE WARNING AGAINST ADDING OR TAKING AWAY

Read Scripture: Revelation 22:18-19
Focus Scripture: Revelation 22:18 (NASB)
"I testify to everyone who hears the words of the prophecy of this book: if anyone adds to them, God will add to him the plagues which are written in this book."

ANECDOTE:

Imagine working on a detailed project with precise instructions, knowing that any changes or mistakes could lead to serious consequences. In Revelation 22, we are given a solemn warning about tampering with God's Word. Any attempt to add to or take away from the words of this prophecy will result in severe consequences.

EXPLANATION:

This passage contains a clear and serious warning from God. John, inspired by the Holy Spirit, warns that anyone who adds to the words of the prophecy will face the plagues written in the book, and anyone who takes away from it will lose their share in the tree of life and the holy city. This warning is directed at those who would distort or misrepresent God's Word, either by adding their own ideas or by removing essential truths.

The book of Revelation is not merely a symbolic or mystical vision— it is the final and complete revelation of God's plan for the end of the age. As such, it must be handled with reverence and care. God's Word is perfect, and any attempt to alter it undermines the authority of Scripture and the truth of God's message.

This warning serves as a reminder of the importance of protecting the integrity of God's Word. It also highlights the serious consequences of distorting Scripture, whether through false teaching, manipulation, or misinterpretation. For believers, it is a call to faithfully study, uphold, and share the truth of God's Word without compromising or changing its message.

APPLICATION:

The warning against adding to or taking away from God's Word challenges us to approach Scripture with reverence and humility. Are we handling God's Word faithfully, or are we tempted to change or compromise its message to fit our own ideas or preferences? This passage encourages us to stay true to the authority of Scripture, trusting that God's Word is complete and perfect as it is.

Are you faithfully handling the Word of God, or are there areas where you may be tempted to compromise or distort its message? Let this passage remind you of the importance of honoring God's Word and of sharing it truthfully with others.

FURTHER READING:

Deuteronomy 4:2, 2 Timothy 3:16-17, Proverbs 30:5-6

PRAYER:

Lord, thank You for the gift of Your Word. Help me to handle it faithfully, with reverence and humility, knowing that it is complete and perfect. Guard my heart against any temptation to add to or take away from Your truth and give me the wisdom to share Your Word with integrity. Amen.

CHALLENGE:

Reflect on how you approach God's Word. Are there areas where you may be tempted to compromise or change its message? Commit to studying Scripture with reverence and sharing it faithfully, trusting that God's Word is perfect and sufficient.

DAY 6: THE PROMISE OF CHRIST'S RETURN

Read Scripture: Revelation 22:20
Focus Scripture: Revelation 22:20 (NASB)
*"He who testifies to these things says, 'Yes, I am com-
ing quickly.' Amen. Come, Lord Jesus."*

ANECDOTE:

Think of the excitement and anticipation you feel when waiting for
a loved one to return after a long time apart. You look forward to their
arrival with joy and eagerness. In Revelation 22, we see a similar anticipation as Jesus promises, "Yes, I am coming quickly," and the response of
John is one of longing: "Come, Lord Jesus."

EXPLANATION:

The promise of Christ's return is one of the central themes of Revelation and the Christian faith. Jesus, the One who testifies to these things,
assures us that He is coming quickly. This doesn't necessarily mean "soon"
in terms of human time, but it emphasizes the sudden and imminent
nature of His return. His coming will be swift, and it will bring the fulfillment of all that has been revealed in the book of Revelation.

For believers, the promise of Christ's return is a source of hope and
joy. It reminds us that no matter what trials or difficulties we face in this
world, Jesus is coming back to establish His eternal kingdom. The response, "Come, Lord Jesus," reflects the longing in the hearts of believers
for the day when Christ will return and make all things right.

This passage also serves as a reminder to live with a sense of urgency
and expectation. Knowing that Jesus could return at any moment should
inspire us to live faithfully, sharing the gospel and preparing our hearts
for His arrival. It's a call to live each day in light of eternity, with our eyes
fixed on the promise of His coming.

APPLICATION:

The promise of Christ's return challenges us to examine how we are living in the present. Are we living with the expectation that Jesus could return at any moment? This passage encourages us to live with hope, joy, and urgency, knowing that our Savior is coming soon. It also invites us to pray, like John, for Christ to come quickly and bring the fulfillment of God's kingdom.

Are you living in eager anticipation of Christ's return? Let this passage remind you of the hope and joy that come from knowing Jesus is coming back and inspire you to live faithfully as you wait for His arrival.

FURTHER READING:

Matthew 24:42-44, 1 Thessalonians 4:16-17, Titus 2:11-13

PRAYER:

Lord Jesus, thank You for the promise that You are coming quickly. Help me to live with a sense of urgency and anticipation, knowing that Your return is near. Fill my heart with hope and joy as I look forward to the day when You will come and make all things right. Come, Lord Jesus! Amen.

CHALLENGE:

Spend time today reflecting on the promise of Christ's return. Are you living with the anticipation that He could come at any moment? Consider how this truth impacts your daily life and ask God to help you live faithfully as you wait for His return.

DAY 7: COME, LORD JESUS

Read Scripture: Revelation 22:21
Focus Scripture: Revelation 22:21 (NASB)
"The grace of the Lord Jesus be with all. Amen."

ANECDOTE:

Imagine the final moments of a long, heartfelt letter. You've shared everything important and now leave the recipient with words of comfort and encouragement. In the final verse of Revelation, John closes with a simple but powerful blessing: "The grace of the Lord Jesus be with all." It's a fitting end to a book filled with both warning and hope, reminding us that God's grace is what sustains us as we wait for Christ's return.

EXPLANATION:

Revelation, a book filled with visions of judgment, victory, and the ultimate triumph of Christ, concludes with a blessing. "The grace of the Lord Jesus be with all." This final verse reminds us that it is by God's grace alone that we are saved, sustained, and secure in the promises of Christ's return. The grace of Jesus is what enables believers to persevere in faith as we live in anticipation of His second coming.

Throughout Revelation, we've seen a picture of the world's brokenness and God's plan for its restoration. As we face trials, persecution, and challenges in this life, it's the grace of the Lord Jesus that gives us strength and hope. John's final words are a reminder that God's grace is available to all who believe, offering forgiveness, comfort, and the promise of eternal life.

The word "Amen" at the end of the verse signifies agreement and affirmation. It's as if John is inviting readers to join in this prayerful desire for God's grace to be upon all who follow Christ. As believers, we cling to this grace, knowing that it is the only way we can remain faithful as we wait for the return of our Savior.

APPLICATION:

The final blessing in Revelation invites us to live in the daily reality of God's grace. Are we relying on His grace to sustain us in our faith and to strengthen us as we face the trials of life? This passage encourages us to rest in the grace of Jesus, knowing that it is through His grace alone that we are saved, sustained, and secure in the hope of His return.

Are you living in the grace of the Lord Jesus? Let this passage remind you that His grace is sufficient for every need, and let it inspire you to live each day with the confidence that His grace is with you, even as you await His return.

FURTHER READING:

2 Corinthians 12:9, Ephesians 2:8-9, Hebrews 4:16

PRAYER:

Lord Jesus, thank You for Your grace that sustains me each day. Help me to rest in Your grace, knowing that it is by Your grace alone that I am saved and strengthened. Thank You for the hope of Your return, and for the promise that Your grace will be with me as I wait. Amen.

CHALLENGE:

Reflect on how the grace of the Lord Jesus is sustaining you in your daily life. Are there areas where you need to rely more on His grace? Take time today to thank God for His grace and to ask Him to strengthen you through it as you live in hope of Christ's return.

WEEK 12: "THE FINAL INVITATION AND WARNING"
BEYOND THE UNVEILING, GOING DEEPER

- How does the final invitation to "come" resonate with your own faith journey?

- What does the warning against adding or taking away from Revelation teach you about God's Word?

- Reflect on Jesus as the Alpha and Omega. How does this affect your trust in His sovereignty?

- How can you respond to the invitation to share the gospel with urgency?

- How does the promise of Jesus' return motivate you to live faithfully?

- How can this chapter encourage you to stand firm in the truth of God's Word?

- How can you use this week's study to invite others to find hope in Christ?

WEEK 13: LIVING IN THE LIGHT OF REVELATION

DAY 1: LIVING WITH HOPE IN CHRIST'S RETURN (TITUS 2:11-14)

DAY 2: ENCOURAGED BY GOD'S SOVEREIGNTY (ISAIAH 46:9-10)

DAY 3: THE URGENCY OF SHARING THE GOSPEL (MATTHEW 28:18-20)

DAY 4: PERSEVERING IN FAITH (HEBREWS 12:1-2)

DAY 5: LIVING WITH AN ETERNAL PERSPECTIVE (COLOSSIANS 3:1-4)

DAY 6: HOLDING FAST TO TRUTH (2 TIMOTHY 3:16-17)

DAY 7: LIVING AS AMBASSADORS OF CHRIST (2 CORINTHIANS 5:18-20)

DAY 1: LIVING WITH HOPE IN CHRIST'S RETURN

Read Scripture: Titus 2:11-14
Focus Scripture: Titus 2:13 (NASB)
"Looking for the blessed hope and the appearing of the glory of our great God and Savior, Christ Jesus."

ANECDOTE:

Have you ever waited for an event you were excited about, counting down the days with anticipation? As believers, we live in constant anticipation of Christ's return, looking forward to the fulfillment of God's promises and the blessed hope we have in Him.

EXPLANATION:

In this passage Paul reminds us that as we live in the grace of God, we are called to look forward to the "blessed hope," the return of our Savior, Jesus Christ. His return is a promise that gives us hope and shapes the way we live today. This blessed hope isn't just a vague wish for the future, but a confident expectation of what God has promised through Christ.

While we wait for Christ's return, we are called to live in a way that reflects our hope. God's grace teaches us to deny ungodliness and worldly desires, and instead to live righteously, eagerly awaiting the appearing of Jesus. This hope should inspire us to live with purpose and faithfulness, knowing that our Savior is coming soon.

For believers, the hope of Christ's return is a source of joy and encouragement. It reminds us that this world is not our final home and that we are living for something far greater: eternity with God.

APPLICATION:

The hope of Christ's return challenges us to live with intentionality and purpose. Are we living each day with the expectation that Jesus could come at any moment? This passage encourages us to live with hope, holiness, and eagerness, knowing that the fulfillment of God's promises is near.

Are you living with the hope of Christ's return in mind? Let this passage remind you of the blessed hope you have in Him, and let it inspire you to live faithfully as you wait for His return.

FURTHER READING:

1 Thessalonians 4:16-17, Philippians 3:20-21, 1 Peter 1:13

PRAYER:

Lord Jesus, thank You for the blessed hope of Your return. Help me to live each day in anticipation of Your coming, and to live in a way that reflects the grace You have shown me. Thank You for the promise of eternity with You, and for the joy that comes from knowing You are coming soon. Amen.

CHALLENGE:

Take time today to reflect on how the hope of Christ's return shapes the way you live. Are there areas of your life where you need to live with more intentionality and purpose? Ask God to help you live in the light of His return.

DAY 2: ENCOURAGED BY GOD'S SOVEREIGNTY

Read Scripture: Isaiah 46:9-10
Focus Scripture: Isaiah 46:10 (NASB)
"Declaring the end from the beginning, and from ancient times things which have not been done, saying, 'My purpose will be established, and I will accomplish all My good pleasure.'"

ANECDOTE:

Think of a time when someone made a plan and saw it through to completion, no matter what obstacles arose. In Isaiah 46, God declares His sovereignty over all of history, assuring us that His purpose will be established and that nothing can thwart His plans.

EXPLANATION:

This passage is a powerful declaration of God's sovereignty. He is not limited by time or circumstance. He declares the end from the beginning, knowing all things and orchestrating history according to His perfect will. God's purpose will be established, and He will accomplish all that He has planned.

For believers, this truth is a great source of encouragement. No matter what happens in the world or in our lives, we can trust that God is in control. His purposes will be fulfilled, and nothing can stand in the way of His will. This includes the ultimate plan of redemption and the return of Christ, as revealed in the book of Revelation.

God's sovereignty should give us confidence and peace, even in uncertain times. We know that He is working all things for good and that His plans cannot fail.

APPLICATION:

The sovereignty of God challenges us to trust Him fully, even when we don't understand what is happening. Are there areas of your life where you're struggling to trust God's plan? This passage encourages us to rest in the knowledge that God's purpose will be established and that He is working all things according to His good pleasure.

Are you trusting in God's sovereignty over your life? Let this passage remind you that God is in control, and that His plans will not fail.

FURTHER READING:

Romans 8:28, Psalm 33:10-11, Proverbs 19:21

PRAYER:

Lord, thank You for Your sovereignty and for the assurance that Your purpose will be accomplished. Help me to trust in Your plans, even when I don't understand, and to rest in the knowledge that You are in control. Thank You for the peace that comes from knowing You are sovereign over all things. Amen.

CHALLENGE:

Reflect on an area of your life where you are struggling to trust God's plan. Surrender that area to Him today, knowing that His purpose will be accomplished, and ask for peace and confidence in His sovereignty.

DAY 3: THE URGENCY OF SHARING THE GOSPEL

Read Scripture: Matthew 28:18-20
Focus Scripture: Matthew 28:19 (NASB)
"Go therefore and make disciples of all the nations, baptizing them in the name of the Father and the Son and the Holy Spirit."

ANECDOTE:

Think of a message so important that it can't wait, something urgent that needs to be shared immediately. In the Great Commission, Jesus gives His disciples an urgent mission: to go into all the world and make disciples, sharing the good news of salvation with everyone.

EXPLANATION:

The Great Commission is the final command Jesus gave to His disciples before ascending into heaven. It is a call to action, urging believers to go into the world and share the gospel, making disciples of all nations. This command is not just for the original disciples but for every believer throughout history.

The urgency of the Great Commission is clear. The message of salvation is too important to keep to ourselves. Jesus has entrusted us with the responsibility of sharing the good news with those who do not yet know Him. We are called to make disciples, baptize them, and teach them to obey all that Jesus commanded.

For believers, the Great Commission is a reminder that our mission is not just to live for ourselves but to reach out to others with the message of hope and salvation. The return of Christ is coming, and we are called to share the gospel with urgency, knowing that every person has the opportunity to come to faith in Him.

APPLICATION:

The urgency of sharing the gospel challenges us to evaluate how we are fulfilling the Great Commission in our own lives. Are we actively sharing our faith with others, or are we hesitant or distracted by other priorities? This passage encourages us to live with a sense of urgency, recognizing that the time is short and the need is great.

Are you living with the urgency of the Great Commission? Let this passage inspire you to share the gospel with those around you, knowing that Jesus has given you the mission to make disciples of all nations.

FURTHER READING:

Acts 1:8, Romans 10:13-15, 2 Timothy 4:2

PRAYER:

Lord, thank You for entrusting me with the mission to share the gospel. Help me to live with a sense of urgency, knowing that the message of salvation is too important to keep to myself. Give me the courage and wisdom to share the good news with those around me, and use me to make disciples for Your kingdom. Amen.

CHALLENGE:

Consider someone in your life who needs to hear the message of salvation. Pray for an opportunity to share the gospel with them this week and ask God for the boldness and wisdom to speak the truth in love.

DAY 4: PERSEVERING IN FAITH

Read Scripture: Hebrews 12:1-2
Focus Scripture: Hebrews 12:1 (NASB)
"Therefore, since we have so great a cloud of witnesses surrounding us, let us also lay aside every encumbrance and the sin which so easily entangles us, and let us run with endurance the race that is set before us."

ANECDOTE:

Imagine running a race with a crowd cheering you on, encouraging you to keep going. In Hebrews 12, we are reminded that we are surrounded by a great cloud of witnesses—those who have gone before us in faith—encouraging us to persevere as we run the race of life with endurance.

EXPLANATION:

This passage calls believers to persevere in faith, likening the Christian life to a race. The "great cloud of witnesses" refers to the faithful believers who have come before us, their lives serving as examples of endurance and faithfulness. As we run our own race, we are encouraged to lay aside every weight that hinders us and the sin that so easily entangles us.

Running the race with endurance requires us to keep our eyes fixed on Jesus, the author and perfecter of our faith. He is our ultimate example, having endured the cross for the joy set before Him. In the same way, we are called to endure trials and challenges, trusting that God is working in us and that the finish line is eternity with Him.

For believers, this passage is a reminder that the Christian life is not always easy, but we are not alone. We are surrounded by the testimony of those who have gone before us, and we have Jesus Himself as our guide and strength.

APPLICATION:

The call to persevere in faith challenges us to examine the things that may be hindering our spiritual race. Are there sins or distractions that are slowing us down? This passage encourages us to lay those things aside and to run with endurance, keeping our eyes fixed on Jesus as we press toward the goal.

Are you running the race of faith with endurance, or are there things weighing you down? Let this passage inspire you to persevere, knowing that you are surrounded by witnesses and empowered by Jesus to finish the race.

FURTHER READING:

Philippians 3:13-14, 2 Timothy 4:7-8, James 1:12

PRAYER:

Lord, thank You for the encouragement to persevere in faith. Help me to lay aside anything that is hindering my spiritual race, and give me the endurance to keep going, even when the path is difficult. Thank You for being my example and my strength as I run the race set before me. Amen.

CHALLENGE:

Reflect on your spiritual race. Are there any sins or distractions that are weighing you down? Commit to laying those things aside and ask God for the strength to persevere in faith.

DAY 5: LIVING WITH AN ETERNAL PERSPECTIVE

Read Scripture: Colossians 3:1-4
Focus Scripture: Colossians 3:2 (NASB)
*"Set your mind on the things above, not
on the things that are on earth."*

ANECDOTE:

Have you ever been so focused on something that everything else fades into the background? In Colossians 3, Paul urges believers to set their minds on things above, to live with an eternal perspective, rather than being consumed by the temporary things of this world.

EXPLANATION:

This passage calls believers to live with their focus on eternal things. Paul reminds us that because we have been raised with Christ, we are called to set our minds on the things above, on the realities of God's kingdom rather than on the temporary things of this world. Our identity is in Christ, and our lives are now hidden with Him, which means that our true home is not here on earth but in heaven.

Living with an eternal perspective means that we prioritize what matters most in God's kingdom—His will, His purposes, and His glory—over the fleeting pursuits of this world. It's a call to live in light of eternity, knowing that when Christ appears, we too will appear with Him in glory.

For believers, this passage is a reminder that the things of this world are temporary and that we are called to live for something far greater: eternity with God. Our decisions, actions, and priorities should reflect this eternal perspective.

APPLICATION:

The call to set our minds on things above challenges us to examine our priorities. Are we focused on temporary, earthly things, or are we living with an eternal perspective? This passage encourages us to align our hearts and minds with God's kingdom and to live in a way that reflects our heavenly citizenship.

Are you living with an eternal perspective? Let this passage remind you to set your mind on the things above, and let it inspire you to live with a focus on God's eternal purposes.

FURTHER READING:

Matthew 6:19-21, 2 Corinthians 4:18, Philippians 3:20-21

PRAYER:

Lord, thank You for the reminder to set my mind on the things above. Help me to live with an eternal perspective, focusing on what matters most in Your kingdom. Thank You for the promise of eternity with You, and for the hope that shapes the way I live today. Amen.

CHALLENGE:

Reflect on your priorities. Are there areas where you are too focused on earthly things? Take time today to shift your perspective and align your heart with God's eternal purposes.

DAY 6: HOLDING FAST TO TRUTH

Read Scripture: 2 Timothy 3:16-17
Focus Scripture: 2 Timothy 3:16 (NASB)
*"All Scripture is inspired by God and profitable for teaching,
for reproof, for correction, for training in righteousness."*

ANECDOTE:

Imagine holding onto a rope as you climb a steep hill. The rope is your lifeline, keeping you from slipping. In 2 Timothy 3, Paul reminds us that Scripture is our lifeline, God's inspired Word that guides us, corrects us, and keeps us grounded in truth.

EXPLANATION:

This passage emphasizes the importance of holding fast to Scripture as the inspired Word of God. Paul reminds Timothy that all Scripture is "God-breathed" and is useful for teaching, rebuking, correcting, and training in righteousness. The Bible is not just a collection of ancient writings—it is the living Word of God, given to guide us in truth and to equip us for every good work.

For believers, this passage is a reminder that Scripture is our ultimate authority. It teaches us how to live according to God's will, corrects us when we go astray, and trains us in righteousness. Holding fast to the truth of God's Word is essential for living a life that is pleasing to Him.

In a world where truth is often distorted or ignored, we are called to stand firm on the truth of Scripture. God's Word is unchanging, and it is through His Word that we are equipped to navigate the challenges of life and to fulfill the calling He has placed on us.

APPLICATION:

The call to hold fast to Scripture challenges us to evaluate how we are engaging with God's Word. Are we studying it regularly, allowing it to teach and guide us, or are we neglecting its importance in our lives? This passage encourages us to be grounded in the truth of Scripture and to allow it to shape the way we live.

Are you holding fast to the truth of God's Word? Let this passage inspire you to deepen your commitment to studying Scripture and to allow it to equip you for every good work.

FURTHER READING:

Psalm 119:105, James 1:22, Hebrews 4:12

PRAYER:

Lord, thank You for the gift of Your Word. Help me to hold fast to the truth of Scripture and to allow it to guide and correct me in every area of my life. Thank You for the wisdom and instruction You provide through Your Word, and for the way it equips me to live for You. Amen.

CHALLENGE:

Consider how you are engaging with God's Word. Are you spending regular time in Scripture, allowing it to shape your life? Commit to deepening your study of the Bible, trusting that it is God's inspired truth.

DAY 7: LIVING AS AMBASSADORS OF CHRIST

Read Scripture: 2 Corinthians 5:18-20
Focus Scripture: 2 Corinthians 5:20 (NASB)
"Therefore, we are ambassadors for Christ, as though
God were making an appeal through us; we beg you
on behalf of Christ, be reconciled to God."

ANECDOTE:

Imagine being appointed as an ambassador, representing your country in a foreign land. As Christians, we are called to be ambassadors for Christ, representing Him to a world in need of reconciliation with God.

EXPLANATION:

In this passage, Paul describes believers as ambassadors for Christ. As ambassadors, we are representatives of Christ, sent into the world to share the message of reconciliation. Through Jesus, God has reconciled the world to Himself, and He has entrusted us with the message of that reconciliation.

Being an ambassador for Christ means that we are called to share the gospel and to live in a way that reflects the character of Jesus. We are His representatives in the world, and through our words and actions, we are making an appeal to others to be reconciled to God. This is a high calling, and it requires us to live with intentionality, knowing that we are reflecting Christ to those around us.

For believers, this passage is a reminder that we have been given a mission. We are not just living for ourselves, we are representing Christ in everything we do. Our lives are a testimony of God's grace and a reflection of His love to a world in need.

APPLICATION:

The call to be an ambassador for Christ challenges us to examine how we are representing Jesus in our daily lives. Are we living in a way that reflects His character and message of reconciliation? This passage encourages us to live intentionally, knowing that we are Christ's representatives, and to share the gospel with those who need to be reconciled to God.

Are you living as an ambassador for Christ? Let this passage remind you of the high calling you have as a representative of Jesus and let it inspire you to live in a way that reflects His love and grace to others.

FURTHER READING:

Matthew 5:14-16, Ephesians 6:20, 1 Peter 2:9

PRAYER:

Lord, thank You for calling me to be Your ambassador. Help me to represent You well in everything I do and to share the message of reconciliation with those around me. Give me the courage and wisdom to speak the truth in love and to live as a reflection of Your grace. Amen.

CHALLENGE:

Reflect on how you are representing Christ in your daily life. Are you living as an ambassador for Him, sharing the message of reconciliation with others? Ask God for opportunities to be His ambassador this week and to represent Him well.

WEEK 13: "LIVING IN THE LIGHT OF REVELATION"

BEYOND THE UNVEILING, GOING DEEPER

- How can living with hope in Christ's return impact your daily decisions?

- In what ways does God's sovereignty strengthen you to face life's challenges?

- Reflect on the urgency of sharing the gospel. How can you make this a priority in your life?

- How can you persevere in your faith, knowing Christ's promises will be fulfilled?

- How does an eternal perspective change your view of temporary difficulties?

- How can you commit to holding fast to the truth of Scripture?

- How can you live as an ambassador of Christ in your community this week?

BONUS WEEK 14:

DANIEL'S SEVENTY WEEKS
AND THE TRIBULATION

I wanted to include a week of devotions based upon Daniel's Seventy Weeks Prophecy. It lays out God's prophetic timeline for the ages. There are actually *eight* devotions that explain the exactness of the Bible's prophetic Word and ties in the time of Daniel, the coming and cutting off of the Messiah, the church age, and the final seven weeks of Daniel's prophetic vision, the seven-year tribulation of Revelation. I hope it helps you to see that God has always had a plan and purpose and in His sovereignty nothing throughout the ages, including our own individual lives have been left to chance.

Day 1: Understanding the Prophecy of Seventy Weeks

Day 2: God's Plan for Israel

Day 3: The Holy City, Jerusalem

Day 4: The Purpose of the Seventy Weeks

Day 5: The Timeline of the Seventy Weeks

Day 6: The Messiah Cut Off

Day 7: The Final Week— The Tribulation

Last Day: The Church Age in Relation to Daniel's Seventy Weeks

DAY 1: UNDERSTANDING THE PROPHECY OF SEVENTY WEEKS

Read Scripture: Daniel 9:24
Focus Scripture: Daniel 9:24 (NASB)
"Seventy weeks have been decreed for your people and your holy city, to finish the transgression, to make an end of sin, to make atonement for iniquity, to bring in everlasting righteousness, to seal up vision and prophecy and to anoint the most holy place."

ANECDOTE:

Imagine receiving a detailed roadmap, but instead of guiding you through cities and roads, it charts the course of history itself. Daniel received such a roadmap, one that outlined God's prophetic plan for His people, Israel, and the world. This vision of "seventy weeks" would span 490 years and culminate in the final redemption and restoration of God's creation.

EXPLANATION:

The seventy weeks mentioned in this prophecy are not weeks of days but weeks of years. Each "week" represents seven years, making the total period 490 years. This prophecy is a timeline that encompasses the history of Israel from the decree to rebuild Jerusalem to the coming of the Messiah and, finally, the seven-year tribulation. The purpose of these weeks is revealed in six key objectives: to finish the transgression, make an end of sin, make atonement for iniquity, bring in everlasting righteousness, seal up vision and prophecy, and anoint the most holy place.

Each of these purposes points to God's ultimate plan for His people and the world. The prophecy highlights the problem of sin and God's solution through His redemptive work. It foretells a time when sin will be dealt with once and for all, and righteousness will reign. This prophecy sets the stage for the coming Messiah and the final judgment upon the earth.

For believers, this prophecy reveals the meticulous nature of God's plan. He has set a timeline for His purposes, and nothing will derail it. The prophecy also points forward to the tribulation and Christ's second coming, events that were still future for Daniel but hold deep significance for us today.

APPLICATION:

The prophecy of seventy weeks challenges us to trust in God's perfect timing and plan. Just as He had a detailed timeline for Israel, He also has a purpose and plan for our lives. The world may seem chaotic, but God is in control, and His plan will unfold exactly as He has decreed. This prophecy also reminds us of the seriousness of sin and the hope of redemption through Christ.

Are you trusting in God's timing and plan for your life? Let this passage remind you that God is sovereign over history and over your life, and that His plan will be accomplished in His perfect timing.

FURTHER READING:

Jeremiah 29:10-14, Isaiah 46:9-10, Ephesians 1:9-11

PRAYER:

Lord, thank You for revealing Your plan for history through Your Word. Help me to trust in Your perfect timing and to rest in the assurance that You are in control. Thank You for the hope of redemption through Christ and for the promise that You will bring Your plans to completion. Amen.

CHALLENGE:

Reflect on areas in your life where you may be struggling to trust God's timing. Surrender those areas to Him in prayer, asking for the patience and faith to trust in His plan.

DAY 2: GOD'S PLAN FOR ISRAEL

Read Scripture: Daniel 9:24
Focus Scripture: Daniel 9:24b (NASB)
"...Seventy weeks have been decreed for
your people and your holy city..."

ANECDOTE:

Imagine a master architect working on a grand blueprint for a city, knowing that every detail must fit perfectly into place. This is how God has planned for His people, Israel. His design is flawless, and His timing is precise. The prophecy of seventy weeks in Daniel is part of this grand design, revealing the future of Israel and how it fits into God's redemptive plan.

EXPLANATION:

The prophecy of seventy weeks is specifically directed to "your people" (Israel) and "your holy city" (Jerusalem). This prophecy reveals that God has not forgotten His covenant with Israel, and He has a specific plan for them. Even as the world seems chaotic, God's sovereign purposes for Israel remain intact.

Throughout history, Israel has been at the center of God's plan. From the calling of Abraham to the establishment of the kingdom of Israel, and through their exile and restoration, Israel's story is intricately woven into the fabric of God's redemptive timeline. The seventy weeks prophecy outlines the final stages of this plan, culminating in the coming of the Messiah and the eventual tribulation, where Israel will once again play a central role.

For believers today, this passage reminds us of the faithfulness of God to His promises. Just as God has been faithful to Israel throughout history, He will remain faithful to all of His promises. The focus on Israel in this prophecy also reminds us to watch and pray for the peace of Jerusalem and for the fulfillment of God's plan for His people.

APPLICATION:

God's plan for Israel challenges us to consider His faithfulness to all of His promises. Are there promises in Scripture that you're waiting to see fulfilled in your life? Just as God's plan for Israel will come to pass, His promises to you will also be fulfilled in His perfect timing. This prophecy also reminds us to pray for Israel and for the peace of Jerusalem as we await the fulfillment of God's redemptive plan.

Are you trusting in God's faithfulness to His promises? Let this passage encourage you to rest in the assurance that just as God's plan for Israel will be fulfilled, His promises for you are also sure.

FURTHER READING:

Romans 11:25-29, Psalm 122:6, Genesis 12:1-3

PRAYER:

Lord, thank You for Your faithfulness to Israel and to all Your promises. Help me to trust in Your plan for my life, even when I don't see the full picture. I pray for the peace of Jerusalem and for the fulfillment of Your promises for Israel and the world. Amen.

CHALLENGE:

Take time today to pray for Israel, asking God to fulfill His plan for His people and to bring peace to Jerusalem. Reflect on how God has been faithful to His promises in your life.

DAY 3: THE HOLY CITY, JERUSALEM

Read Scripture: Daniel 9:24
Focus Scripture: Daniel 9:24b (NASB)
"Seventy weeks have been decreed for your people and your holy city…"

ANECDOTE:

Imagine a city that has witnessed centuries of history, from the rise and fall of kingdoms to the movements of great leaders. Jerusalem stands as one of the most historically and spiritually significant cities in the world. For centuries, it has been the heart of God's people, and in the prophecy of Daniel's seventy weeks, it plays a pivotal role in the fulfillment of God's plan.

EXPLANATION:

Jerusalem is called "the holy city" because of its central role in God's redemptive purposes. It was the place where the temple stood, where God's presence was uniquely manifest among His people. The seventy weeks prophecy makes it clear that Jerusalem remains central to God's plan for the future, especially as it concerns the return of Christ and the establishment of His kingdom.

Throughout history Jerusalem has been a focal point of spiritual warfare and a symbol of God's covenant with His people. It has been conquered, destroyed, and rebuilt numerous times, yet it remains at the heart of biblical prophecy. As we look ahead to the tribulation, Jerusalem will once again become the center stage for the fulfillment of prophetic events, including the rise of the Antichrist and the eventual return of Christ.

This prophecy reminds us that the story of Jerusalem is not over. Just as it was the city of kings in the past, it will one day be the city of the ultimate King, Jesus Christ. The "holy city" will be the place where God's promises are fulfilled, where sin will be defeated, and where righteousness will reign.

APPLICATION:

The significance of Jerusalem in biblical prophecy challenges us to see the world through God's eyes, understanding that His plans are not just for individuals but for nations and cities as well. As we watch events unfold in the world, we should keep our eyes on Jerusalem and pray for the fulfillment of God's promises. This passage also reminds us that just as God's plan for Jerusalem will be fulfilled, so too will His promises in our lives.

Are you praying for God's purposes to be fulfilled in Jerusalem and in the world? Let this passage remind you that God's plan for the holy city is unfolding, and that we are called to pray for its peace and for the return of the King.

FURTHER READING:

Zechariah 8:3, Isaiah 2:2-4, Psalm 48:1-2

PRAYER:

Lord, thank You for Your faithfulness to Jerusalem, the city of Your promises. Help me to see the world through Your eyes and to pray for the peace of Jerusalem. As I watch for the fulfillment of Your plan, give me the faith to trust in Your timing. Amen.

CHALLENGE:

Take time today to pray specifically for the city of Jerusalem, asking God to bring about His peace and purpose for this city that remains at the heart of biblical prophecy.

DAY 4: THE PURPOSE OF THE SEVENTY WEEKS

Read Scripture: Daniel 9:24
Focus Scripture: Daniel 9:24c (NASB)
"To finish the transgression, to make an end of sin, to make atonement for iniquity, to bring in everlasting righteousness, to seal up vision and prophecy and to anoint the most holy place."

ANECDOTE:

Imagine an artist unveiling a masterpiece, with every stroke of the brush serving a purpose in bringing the vision to completion. God's prophecy of seventy weeks is like a masterpiece, where every moment is designed to accomplish His ultimate plan for humanity. This prophecy reveals six key objectives that God will fulfill as part of His redemptive plan.

EXPLANATION:

The prophecy of the seventy weeks is not just a timeline, it's a revelation of God's plan to deal with the problem of sin and to bring about His kingdom. The six objectives laid out in Daniel 9:24 summarize God's redemptive mission for Israel and the world:

To finish the transgression. This refers to the culmination of Israel's rebellion against God. God will bring an end to their transgression through His judgment and ultimately through their redemption.

To make an end of sin. Sin's reign over humanity will come to a final end. This was initiated at the cross and will be fully realized at Christ's second coming.

To make atonement for iniquity. Jesus' death on the cross provided atonement for the sins of the world. This is the heart of the gospel and central to God's plan for redemption.

To bring in everlasting righteousness. When Jesus returns, He will establish His kingdom, bringing a reign of righteousness that will last forever.

To seal up vision and prophecy. This means that all the visions and prophecies concerning Israel and the end times will be fulfilled and completed.

To anoint the most holy place. The temple in Jerusalem (or more broadly, the presence of God among His people) will be restored and anointed, ushering in the eternal reign of Christ.

This passage reveals the depth and beauty of God's plan to address the problem of sin and to establish His righteous kingdom. For believers, it reminds us that God is not only working to bring about our salvation but also to bring the entire world under His righteous rule.

APPLICATION:

The purpose of the seventy weeks challenges us to see the bigger picture of God's plan for redemption. Are we focused on our daily struggles, or are we seeing our lives in light of God's eternal purpose? This prophecy encourages us to trust in God's plan, knowing that He is working to bring an end to sin, to establish righteousness, and to fulfill all that He has promised.

Are you living with the expectation of God's ultimate plan? Let this passage remind you that God's purpose is being fulfilled and that you are part of His redemptive story.

FURTHER READING:
Romans 11:25-27, Isaiah 53:5-6, Hebrews 9:24-28

PRAYER:
Lord, thank You for revealing Your plan to deal with sin and to bring in everlasting righteousness. Help me to trust in Your purpose and to live with the hope of Your return. Thank You for the atonement that You provided through Jesus, and for the promise of everlasting righteousness. Amen.

CHALLENGE:

Reflect on how God's redemptive plan gives meaning to your life and struggles. Take time to thank God for His plan of salvation and to ask Him to help you live with the assurance that His purpose will be fulfilled.

DAY 5: THE TIMELINE OF THE SEVENTY WEEKS

Read Scripture: Daniel 9:25
Focus Scripture: Daniel 9:25 (NASB)
"So you are to know and discern that from the issuing of a decree to restore and rebuild Jerusalem until Messiah the Prince there will be seven weeks and sixty-two weeks; it will be built again, with plaza and moat, even in times of distress."

ANECDOTE:

Imagine waiting for a long-anticipated event, with a countdown marking the days. You can see each step along the way, and with every passing moment, the excitement builds. In Daniel 9:25, God provides a detailed timeline, marking out significant milestones from the decree to rebuild Jerusalem all the way to the coming of the Messiah.

EXPLANATION:

This verse lays out the prophetic timeline of the seventy weeks. The seventy weeks are broken into three parts:

Seven weeks (49 years): This period refers to the time from the issuing of the decree to rebuild Jerusalem to the completion of the rebuilding process. Historical records confirm that Jerusalem was indeed rebuilt during this time, though it faced many obstacles and challenges.

Sixty-two weeks (434 years): This additional period extends from the rebuilding of Jerusalem until the coming of the Messiah. These 434 years lead up to the ministry and arrival of Jesus Christ. This prophecy is incredibly precise, as it points to the time when Jesus would enter Jerusalem (often associated with His triumphal entry) and be revealed as the Messiah.

One week (seven years): The final week (which will be addressed later) refers to the future tribulation period.

God's prophecy in Daniel is remarkable for its accuracy. It predicted with great precision the time of the Messiah's arrival, which was fulfilled in Jesus Christ. This timeline demonstrates the meticulous nature of God's plan, showing that every event in history unfolds according to His divine purpose.

For believers, this passage is a reminder that God is sovereign over time. He knows the end from the beginning, and every moment of history is part of His perfect plan. The prophecy of the seventy weeks is not just a testament to God's foresight, but also to His faithfulness in fulfilling His promises.

APPLICATION:

The timeline of the seventy weeks challenges us to trust in God's timing, even when we don't see how everything fits together. Are there moments in your life when you've struggled to understand God's plan or timing? This passage encourages us to have faith in God's perfect timing, knowing that just as He fulfilled His promises concerning the Messiah, He will fulfill every promise He has made to us.

Are you trusting in God's timing and plan for your life? Let this passage remind you that God is never late and that His purposes will be fulfilled right on time.

FURTHER READING:

Galatians 4:4-5, Ecclesiastes 3:1-11, 2 Peter 3:8-9

PRAYER:

Lord, thank You for revealing Your perfect timeline for the coming of the Messiah. Help me to trust in Your timing for my own life, knowing that You are sovereign over every moment. Thank You for being faithful to Your promises and for the hope that comes from knowing You are in control of all things. Amen.

CHALLENGE:

Reflect on areas in your life where you may be struggling to trust God's timing. Surrender those areas to Him in prayer, asking for the patience and faith to trust in His perfect plan.

DAY 6: THE MESSIAH CUT OFF

Read Scripture: Daniel 9:26
Focus Scripture: Daniel 9:26a (NASB)
*"Then after the sixty-two weeks the Messiah will be cut
off and have nothing, and the people of the prince who
is to come will destroy the city and the sanctuary."*

ANECDOTE:

Think of a moment when something unexpected and devastating happened, something that seemed completely contrary to your hopes and plans. When Jesus, the long-awaited Messiah, was crucified, it shocked many. His followers expected Him to establish an earthly kingdom immediately, but instead, He was "cut off." Yet in this tragic moment, God's plan of salvation was being fulfilled in ways far beyond what anyone could imagine.

EXPLANATION:

Daniel 9:26 reveals that after the 62 weeks (which follow the initial seven weeks), the Messiah would be "cut off." This refers to the crucifixion of Jesus Christ. His death was not an accident; it was part of God's redemptive plan for the world. When the Messiah was "cut off," He had "nothing." He was rejected by His people, abandoned by His disciples, and crucified as a criminal. Yet, through His death, Jesus secured salvation for all who would believe.

The second part of the prophecy reveals that the people of the coming prince would destroy the city (Jerusalem) and the sanctuary (the temple). This was fulfilled in AD 70 when the Romans, under the command of General Titus, destroyed Jerusalem and the temple. This was a significant event in Jewish history and is directly tied to the rejection of the Messiah.

While the prophecy foretells these devastating events, it also points to the hope that comes through Jesus' sacrifice. His death, though tragic, was the ultimate victory over sin. It opened the way for redemption, not just for Israel but for all nations.

For believers, this passage is a reminder of the cost of our salvation. Jesus, the Messiah, was "cut off" so that we could be reconciled to God. His sacrifice was the turning point in history, fulfilling God's plan of salvation.

APPLICATION:

The Messiah being "cut off" challenges us to reflect on the significance of Jesus' sacrifice. Are we living in gratitude for the price that was paid for our salvation? This passage encourages us to consider the depth of God's love, demonstrated through the death of His Son. It also reminds us that even in the most unexpected and difficult moments, God's plan is being fulfilled.

Are you living in light of the sacrifice that Jesus made for you? Let this passage remind you of the cost of your salvation and inspire you to live a life of gratitude and faithfulness.

FURTHER READING:

Isaiah 53:3-5, Matthew 27:45-50, Romans 5:6-8

PRAYER:

Lord, thank You for the sacrifice of Jesus, the Messiah, who was "cut off" for my sake. Help me to live in gratitude for the price He paid and to remember that His death opened the way for my salvation. Thank You for Your perfect plan and for the hope that comes through Christ's victory over sin. Amen.

CHALLENGE:

Take time today to reflect on the significance of Jesus' death. Consider the price He paid for your salvation, and express your gratitude in prayer and in how you live.

DAY 7: THE FINAL WEEK—
THE TRIBULATION

Read Scripture: Daniel 9:27
Focus Scripture: Daniel 9:27 (NASB)

*"And he will make a firm covenant with the many for one week,
but in the middle of the week he will put a stop to sacrifice and
grain offering; and on the wing of abominations will come one
who makes desolate, even until a complete destruction, one that
is decreed, is poured out on the one who makes desolate."*

ANECDOTE:

Consider the tension that builds in the final moments of a suspenseful story, the moment when everything hangs in the balance. The final week in Daniel's prophecy is like this climactic moment. This is the seven-year tribulation, a period of intense trials, deception, and judgment before the final return of Christ.

EXPLANATION:

The last "week" in Daniel's prophecy refers to a seven-year period commonly understood as the tribulation. This verse highlights a covenant made by a future ruler (often identified as the Antichrist) with "the many," which likely refers to Israel and possibly other nations. This ruler will appear to bring peace by establishing a covenant, but midway through the seven years, he will break it. He will "put a stop to sacrifice and grain offering," signaling a betrayal of the peace he once promised.

At the midpoint of the tribulation, the Antichrist will commit the "abomination of desolation," a desecration of the temple that will signal the beginning of the Great Tribulation, the final three and a half years of intense suffering. This period will be marked by unprecedented tribulation, as described in the book of Revelation, with the world reeling from God's judgment and Satan's deception.

Yet even in this dark time, there is hope. The prophecy concludes with the assurance that the one who brings desolation (the Antichrist) will face complete destruction. God's judgment will be poured out on him, and Jesus Christ will return to defeat evil and establish His eternal kingdom.

For believers, this passage is a reminder that no matter how dark the times may seem, God's plan will prevail. The tribulation is a time of judgment, but it is also a time of preparation for the ultimate triumph of Christ and the fulfillment of God's promises.

APPLICATION:

The prophecy of the final week (the tribulation) challenges us to be watchful and prepared. Are we living with the awareness of Christ's imminent return, or are we distracted by the cares of this world? This passage encourages us to live with urgency, knowing that God's judgment is real, but so is His offer of salvation through Jesus. It also reminds us that no matter how chaotic the world may become, God's plan will be fulfilled, and His victory is sure.

Are you living with the expectation of Christ's return? Let this passage remind you that the tribulation will not last forever. Jesus is coming, and He will bring an end to evil and establish His righteous kingdom.

FURTHER READING:

Matthew 24:15-22, Revelation 13:1-10, 2 Thessalonians 2:3-10

PRAYER:

Lord, thank You for revealing the truth about the future in Your Word. Help me to live with the expectation of Your return and to trust that even in the darkest times, Your plan will prevail. Thank You for the promise of Your victory over evil and for the hope of Your eternal kingdom. Amen.

CHALLENGE:

Reflect on how the knowledge of the coming tribulation and Christ's return affects the way you live. Are there areas of your life where you need to be more watchful or urgent in sharing the gospel? Ask God to help you live with purpose and readiness as you wait for His return.

DAY 8: THE CHURCH AGE IN RELATION TO DANIEL'S SEVENTY WEEKS

Read Scripture: Matthew 28:18-20
Scripture Focus: Matthew 28:19-20; *"Go therefore and make disciples of all nations, baptizing them in the name of the Father, the Son, and the Holy Spirit; teaching them to observe all that I have commanded you; and I will be with you always until the end of the age."*

ANECDOTE:

Imagine watching a play with multiple acts. At the end of one act, the curtain falls, signaling a pause before the next act begins. During the intermission, a new storyline begins to develop. In Daniel's prophecy of seventy weeks, the curtain fell after the Messiah was cut off, but the story didn't end there. This intermission marks the beginning of a new era: the Church Age, the dispensation of the Holy Spirit.

EXPLANATION:

The seventy weeks of Daniel (490 years) are focused on God's plan for Israel. The prophecy marks out 69 weeks (483 years) from the decree to rebuild Jerusalem until the coming of the Messiah. When Jesus was "cut off" at His crucifixion, the prophetic timeline for Israel paused. The events of the final week (the seven-year tribulation) are still future. But in this gap between the 69th and 70th week, God's focus shifted from Israel to the Church, ushering in what we now call the Church Age.

This period began with the outpouring of the Holy Spirit at Pentecost (Acts 2) and continues today. During this time, the gospel has spread to the nations, and the Church (the body of Christ) has grown. God's plan for Israel is still in place, but He is now working primarily through the Church to accomplish His redemptive purposes.

This "intermission" gap in the seventy weeks prophecy is a display of God's grace. Instead of moving directly into the final judgment (the tribulation), God has extended this period to gather people from every nation into His kingdom through the work of the Holy Spirit. We live in the dispensation of grace, where both Jews and Gentiles can respond to the gospel and become part of God's family.

The Church Age will end with the rapture of the Church, after which the final week (the seven-year tribulation) will begin, signaling the resumption of God's focus on Israel and the fulfillment of the remaining prophetic events.

APPLICATION:

The Church Age challenges us to recognize the significance of our times. Are we making the most of this period of grace, knowing that the tribulation will come? This period is an opportunity for the gospel to spread and for people to come to Christ before the final judgment. It encourages us to live with urgency and purpose, knowing that this age will one day come to an end.

Are you living with an awareness of the Church Age and the opportunity it provides to share the gospel? Let this time in history inspire you to make the most of every opportunity to share the message of salvation before the final events of Daniel's prophecy unfold.

FURTHER READING:

Romans 11:25-29, Acts 2:1-4, 2 Peter 3:8-9

PRAYER:

Lord, thank You for the grace You have extended during this time of the Church Age. Help me to make the most of this season, sharing the gospel with those who need to hear it. Thank You for Your perfect plan and for the opportunity we have to be part of Your work in this time. Amen.

CHALLENGE:

Reflect on how you're using the opportunities God has given you in this age of grace. Are there people in your life who need to hear the gospel? Ask God to give you boldness to share His message and to live with an awareness of our times.

BONUS WEEK 14: "DANIEL'S SEVENTY WEEKS AND THE TRIBULATION"

BEYOND THE UNVEILING, GOING DEEPER

- How does the prophecy of Daniel's seventy weeks deepen your understanding of God's timeline?

- What can you learn about God's faithfulness to Israel through this prophecy?

- How does this week's study inspire your trust in God's plan for the future?

- Reflect on the purpose of the seventy weeks. How does this affect your view of end-times events?

- How can the events of the final week increase your desire for holiness and readiness?

- How does understanding the tribulation period challenge you to strengthen your faith?

- How can you prepare spiritually for the fulfillment of God's prophetic promises?

DEAR READER,

This book concludes a three-part devotional series:
Foundations of Faith
The Roman Road
Revelation Unveiled

My goal throughout these devotionals has been to present the essential doctrines of the Christian faith in a way that is engaging, encouraging, and equipping. It is my sincere desire that both new and seasoned believers grow in their faith in Christ and deepen their understanding of what it means to be a follower of Jesus.

God has called each of us to a higher purpose in this world. As 1 Peter 2:9 reminds us: *"But you are A CHOSEN RACE, A royal PRIESTHOOD, A HOLY NATION, A PEOPLE FOR God's OWN POSSESSION, so that you may proclaim the excellencies of Him who has called you out of darkness into His marvelous light."* (NASB) It is crucial for us as believers to understand what it means to be saved and to grasp the doctrines that shape our faith.

The word *doctrine* may seem daunting, something reserved for preachers or theologians, but doctrine is vital for our spiritual growth and maturity in Christ. My hope is that these devotionals have been presented in a way that is accessible, allowing you to absorb the truth of God's Word and apply it to your life, one day at a time, without feeling overwhelmed.

I pray that *Revelation Unveiled* has blessed you, and if you haven't already, I encourage you to continue your journey through *Foundations of Faith* and *The Roman Road*. Each step in these devotionals is designed to help you grow in your walk with the Lord and deepen your understanding of His calling on your life.

Thank you for joining me in this journey. I am praying for you, that you will discover your God-ordained calling in Christ, and that you will move forward in faith, filled with the Holy Spirit, to accomplish all that God has for you.

For the exaltation of Christ,
Dr. Ralph Jenkins
Jehovah Jireh Ministries

Jehovah Jireh Ministries was founded in 2019 by Dr. Ralph and Tammy Jenkins with the mission to bring the gospel to people groups around the world. We focus on planting churches, training pastors, and holding revivals and crusades wherever God leads us. Currently, much of our work is concentrated in India and Pakistan, where we have witnessed over 25,000 people come to Christ since the ministry began.

Jehovah Jireh Ministries operates prayer and conference centers in both India and Pakistan, where we equip national pastors to preach the gospel and shepherd their congregations. Lord willing, we plan to establish Jehovah Jireh Ministry Bible Colleges in both countries by 2025.

We also run a Children's Home in India, where we provide for the children's physical needs while teaching them the Word of God. We are currently working on building a new children's home in India and expanding this mission into Pakistan. God has opened remarkable doors in both countries, allowing us to reach the "least of these" with the love of Christ.

In addition to our work in India and Pakistan, we partner with the Roma (Gypsy) people in Romania and are prayerfully building a ministry presence in the UK.

The needs are immense, but we trust that the Lord will provide for all that He has called us to do. As it says in Mark 16:15, "And He said to them, 'Go into all the world and preach the gospel to all creation.'" Wherever He leads, we will follow.

By purchasing our devotionals, you are not only being blessed spiritually, but you are also supporting the mission of Jehovah Jireh Ministries. Your contribution helps us bring the gospel to the nations, and for that, we are both humbled and grateful.

Until He Comes, We Must Go,
Dr. Ralph Jenkins
www.jehovahjirehministries.com

www.ingramcontent.com/pod-product-compliance
Lightning Source LLC
Chambersburg PA
CBHW030412130626
46549CB00004B/1748